New Orleans
Orleans
in the
SIXTIES

New Orleans
in the
SIXTIES

Mary Lou Widmer

Foreword by Jerry Romig

Pelican Publishing Company
GRETNA 2000

The word "Pelican" and the depiction of a pelican are trademarks of
Pelican Publishing Company, Inc., and are registered in the
U.S. Patent and Trademark Office.

Library of Congress Cataloging-in-Publication Data

Widmer, Mary Lou, 1926-
    New Orleans in the sixties / Mary Lou Widmer ; foreword by Jerry Romig
        p. cm.
    ISBN 1-56554-718-7 (hc : alk. paper)
    1. New Orleans (La.)—History—20th century. 2. New Orleans (La.)—Social life and
customs—20th century. 3. Popular culture—Louisiana—New Orleans—History—20th
century. 4. Nineteen sixties. I. Title: New Orleans in the '60s. II. Title.

F379.N557 W52 2000
976.3'35063—dc21
                                                                                    99-057268

Printed in the United States of America
Published by Pelican Publishing Company, Inc.
1000 Burmaster Street, Gretna, Louisiana 70053

This book is lovingly dedicated to my husband, Al: my chauffeur, my go-for, my instant recall expert, proposer of research resources, tireless helpmate, and my most enthusiastic fan

CONTENTS

Foreword

CHARLES DICKENS WOULD HAVE LOVED NEW ORLEANS in the '60s! The "best of times, the worst of times."

And surely, Sir Charles would have enjoyed the company of Mary Lou Widmer for the two have much in common. Writers both, chronicling the life and times of things so dear to them.

Mary Lou brings us through our beloved Crescent City and the sixties in her best style. Thorough. Warm. Compassionate. Colorful. Totally memorable. For anyone born in the 30s, a read through New Orleans in the Sixties will prove both troubling and triumphant. She reminds us expertly of the sorrowing moments of a President's assassination, of the scores of young New Orleanians who went off to a senseless death in Vietnam. We relive the dreadfully long night of Hurricane Betsy and the seemingly endless trial of school integration.

We're there for the joys of Pontchartrain Beach, the coming of a team called "The Saints," the race to the moon and the role that our city and its craftsmen played in that race at a place called Michoud. We're reminded of the ever-pleasant Mayor Vic Schiro who never met a pair of scissors or cut an opening ribbon he didn't love! She brings us back to the glory days of local TV and catalogs the names of stars who kept us ever fascinated by their talents . . . the likes of Nash and Terry, Wayne and Mel . . . and the teen dance master, John Pela. Who needed cable?

The quintessential Widmer touch takes us through this turbulent yet treasure-filled decade in an organized, easy-to-read style. For fellow parents, she reminds us that ours was a truly hectic responsibility. We had to rear ever-questioning teenagers through racial hatred at home, national turmoil of the worst kind and international divisiveness and war and convince them that it was all going to turn out just fine. And fortunately for most, it did.

Mary Lou offers an expert analysis of the school integration crisis, reminding us of how two small Ninth Ward elementary schools were selected as the unlucky lottery losers of the times. We're there as a handful of frightened young black children are escorted to class by federal marshals through an ugly torrent of bitter racist rhetoric.

Yet it worked as only things like that can in New Orleans. It may have been ugly but it was peaceful and there were places in America that struggled through similar crises and failed miserably.

She brings into full focus all of the players in the coming of professional football to our town. The Saints! David Dixon asking the Archbishop for his "blessing" of the name and His Excellency's delightful reply. Young Saints' owner John Mecom. That marvelous kickoff at our first league game and a more marvelous return for a touchdown. There was Al Hirt, the best of cheerleaders. Tulane Sugar Bowl Stadium, where parking was never a problem. You simply found an uptown friend who had a driveway. She brings us through the planning for the superdome. She tells us how Governor McKeithen craftily enjoined all of Louisiana into supporting a statewide bond issue to pay for this most remarkable of buildings.

Mayor Schiro gets a lot of Widmer ink in this, the latest chronicle of our times. And rightfully so. Victor Hugo Schiro was a very good mayor. He kept the peace, he was a builder, a social butterfly of the best kind. He thrilled at being at the opening of a new business, large or small. He held a pair of scissors like no other mayor. Ribbon-cuttings were a Schiro symbol. Times for Mayor Vic were always good and with every snip of the scissors, there were more jobs for our people. All of us who knew him will remember his beloved Sunny, a first lady of the highest rank. Strangely, he was never given due credit for the positive things he did for racial harmony, including giving black citizens their first really prominent role in city government.

My first read through New Orleans in the Sixties was also personally penetrating. I was very much a part of the broadcast scene then, as a production coordinator at WDSU-TV and eventually, as that station's program director, editorial writer, and vice president for programming. How well I recall, as Mary Lou does in this book, Bill Slatter's incredibly timed interview with presidential assassin Lee Harvey Oswald. Bill was producing a nightly radio call-in program and on this particular night he invited Oswald as his guest. My reaction on hearing that Bill was guesting Oswald was one of dismay. Why, I wondered, would Bill give the guy good air time to promote such a stupid cause? Little did I know!

Oswald had been distributing leaflets outside the old International Trade Mart Building (since torn down and now part of the huge complex that is the Sheraton Hotel). How odd a moment! Oswald promoting Marxism and "Fair Play for Cuba" just steps away from where the late Clay Shaw held court as the Trade Mart's executive director. The author does an excellent re-telling of Jim Garrison's futile (foolish?) Criminal Court presentation of "the Conspiracy theory" and of bringing Mr. Shaw to trial.

The Sixties. All of it (at least, the part we have all played, lived, suffered and/or laughed through) is here for the seeing and the telling. The bitterness of Vietnam and the political trickery of the Gulf of Tonkin Resolution, the first made-for TV war that brought down a president and split up families by the thousands. The astronauts. Alan B. Shepard, Jr. The first manned space flight. Vatican II and the opening of the church windows across the world by Pope John XXIII. Betsy, the hurricane that made Alec Gifford a news star and Nash Roberts an icon. The building of the University of New Orleans (LSUNO in the '60s). The growth of Mardi Gras. Of Bacchus and Endymion. Of doubloons and the coming of the carnival to Metairie.

I sense that Mary Lou thoroughly enjoyed this latest literary project. There's so much of her in it. So much to remember. And she does it in a way that helps all of us recall what it was like. Times when our kids were so young, so involved. Tough times, to be sure. Wonderful years for certain. The Sixties. Thanks for the memories, Mary Lou.

Jerry Romig

Preface

THE DECADE OF THE SIXTIES began and ended with a bang. In 1961, four little black girls were integrated into the all-white public schools of New Orleans, and in 1963, the youngest president in our country's history was killed by an assassin's bullet on a sunny November morning in Dallas, Texas. At the end of the decade, in 1969, Neil Armstrong fulfilled President Kennedy's dream by stepping on the moon and declaring it a "giant leap for mankind."

The decade of the sixties was one that confounded America like no period ever before. It was a tumultuous, threatening, liberating, bloody time which seemed about to change the world. It ushered in a storm of social change and enormous tension. It was a time of expansion of the suburbs and the reconstruction of Poydras Street with the Rivergate anchoring one end and the first signs of Superdome construction at the other. It was the time of the emergence of some of the biggest buildings in the city, of the super krewes, and of tourism as the city's major concern.

It was a decade when orchestras gave way to Rock & Roll groups, when dancing took the shape of the Twist and the Frugue, and when youth, women, and blacks all clamored for rights and acceptance.

Integration was happening everywhere, not only in schools, but in public places and city government. According to past mayor Moon Landrieu, "New Orleans came out of the sixties pretty well. Though there were riots in other cities with large black populations like Watts, Detroit, and New York, there were none here."

It was not a Golden Age, but we weathered it well, and emerged the better for having defeated the Riverfront Expressway, triumphed over the opponents of the Domed Stadium, obtained a franchise in the NFL, reinvented Poydras Street, connected with the West Bank and St. Tammany Parish, and expanded the suburbs. All in all, the sixties offered some giant leaps for New Orleans.

11

Acknowledgments

MANY THANKS to Peggy Scott Laborde of WYES-TV for sharing information and suggesting sources for pictures. Thanks to Marion A. Lanasa, Jr., Director of Public Affairs, Lockheed Martin for information about the space program and the photo of the Saturn rocket booster. Thanks to Wayne Everard at the New Orleans Public Library, Sally Stassi at the Historic New Orleans Collection, Nancy Burris at the Times Picayune Publishing Company, and Florence Jumonville at the Earl K. Long Library, and a special thanks to reference librarian Pamela Arceneaux at the Williams Research Center, for last-minute research. Thanks to William E. Borah, attorney, for slides and to Curtis and Davis, architects, for photos. Thanks to the Marianite sisters for pictures from their yearbooks. Thanks to photographers Tracy Clouatre and Michael P. Smith. And to my many friends who loaned me pictures from their personal collections.

New Orleans
in the
SIXTIES

President John F. Kennedy rode in a convertible with Governor Jimmie Davis and Mayor Victor Schiro in 1962 when he came to dedicate the Nashville Street Wharf. (Courtesy Times Picayune *Publishing Company*)

CHAPTER ONE

They Called
it Camelot

"He didn't even have the satisfaction of being killed for civil rights . . . it had to be some silly little Communist."
                                                          Jacquelyn Kennedy

"At night, before we went to bed, Jack liked to play some records . . . The lines he loved to hear were: 'Don't let it be forgot, that once there was a spot, for one brief shining moment that was known as Camelot.'"
                                                          Jacquelyn Kennedy

THE DOOR TO MY NOONTIME STUDY HALL flew open and one of my students put her head around it. Her face was ashen. "President Kennedy has been shot!" she said. The class of 12-year-old girls looked up from their homework and gasped. Some wept. A pall fell over the group. It was Friday, November 22, 1963.

On Sunday, November 24, the body of the president lay in state beneath the Capitol rotunda. We saw queues of a quarter of a million Americans waiting in the cold to pay homage to their slain leader. Somewhere in that line was my friend's son, who was attending Georgetown University.

At the funeral, our future Archbishop Hannan, then Auxiliary Bishop of Washington, read from the third chapter of Ecclesiastes, which was the president's favorite, "There is an appointed time for everything . . . a time to be born, and a time to die . . ." We watched in silence as a little boy in a blue coat saluted his father's flag-draped casket.

Over the weekend, my husband and I and our two children, like families all over the country, sat before our television set and saw clips of Lee Harvey Oswald, a native New Orleanian, at the police station after he'd been arrested in a movie house in Dallas. Then, only 45 hours later, we saw him grimace as he was shot on live television by Dallas nightclub owner Jack Ruby (Rubinstein) as he was being taken from the Dallas city jail to the county jail.

President Kennedy addressed New Orleanians at the dedication of the Nashville Street Wharf. Seated along the dais to his left were Governor Jimmie Davis and Mayor Victor Schiro. (Courtesy Historic New Orleans Collection, Museum/Research Center, Acc. No. 1986.127.19)

LEE HARVEY OSWALD, A NAME WE WOULD NEVER FORGET

In between scenes of the three-mile funeral procession to Arlington National Cemetery, we saw clips of Lee Harvey Oswald in the summer of 1963, August 9, to be exact, in New Orleans, handing out literature on *Fair Play for Cuba* across the street from the old International Trade Mart Building. Considered little more than a news curiosity at the time, he'd been photographed and, later that evening, interviewed on WDSU by Bill Slatter, where he'd admitted to being a Marxist, but not a Communist. On August 23, 1963, Oswald was on a program on WDSU radio called *Conversation Carte Blanche*, just 90 days before the assassination of the president. His comments were of little consequence and were soon forgotten, until the news broke that he was the alleged assassin of the president. Then the WDSU tape was sent to New York and broadcast nationwide.

LOSS OF A YOUNG AND VIGOROUS LEADER

Whether we had voted for Kennedy or not, most of us thought of him as a friend, a man we could talk to. He never projected an image of an unapproachable leader. Perhaps it was his energy and sense of humor that made him seem so accessible. A young and vigorous president, he understood the youth of the country, their restlessness, and their demands. He loved the Camelot story, and undoubtedly hoped that his administration would be somewhat like that mythological place where all wrongs were righted and justice prevailed.

LEE HARVEY OSWALD'S BACKGROUND

Unlike the President, Oswald was buried ignominiously in a hastily dug grave in Fort Worth's Rose Hill Cemetery. The only mourners were his mother, his widow, his two baby daughters, and his brother Robert. No friends. No pallbearers— seven newsmen did the job.

Lee Harvey Oswald was born in New Orleans shortly after his father died of a heart attack. His brother, Robert, recalls how he slept beside Lee in a New Orleans orphanage, where his mother had put them. His uncle, Charles Murret of New Orleans, in an interview for *The Times-Picayune*, said he'd offered to take them in, but his wife didn't get along with her sister, Margarite (Oswald's mother). The length of their stay in the orphanage is uncertain, but Lee was later back with his mother and brother, and the family eventually moved to Fort Worth, Texas. After moving back to New Orleans, Lee attended both Beauregard Junior High and Warren Easton High School.

They also lived for a time in New York City, where Oswald was a poor student and a chronic truant. A psychiatric report in his student days stated that he had schizophrenic tendencies and was potentially dangerous. Nevertheless, he spent time in the Marine Corps, and then lived for thirty-three months in Russia, trying, unsuccessfully, to gain citizenship. During this time he married a hospital pharmacist, Marina Prusakova. Then, in 1962, he and his wife and baby returned to the United States and settled in the Dallas-Fort Worth area.

In April 1963, when he could find no work in Fort Worth, he came to New Orleans and visited his aunt and uncle, Lillian and Charles Murret. He asked if they could put him up for a few days until he could find work. It was the first time the Murrets had seen anyone in the Oswald family in years. Eventually, Oswald found a job with a New Orleans coffee processor.

Lee Harvey Oswald distributed pamphlets on "Fair Play for Cuba" outside the old International Trade Mart building just ninety days before the assassination of President Kennedy. (Courtesy WWL-TV)

Because it was a slow news day, Bill Slatter of WDSU radio asked Oswald to come to the station to be interviewed. He admitted that he was a Marxist, but not a Communist. (Courtesy WWL-TV)

Marina and her baby had stayed in Texas with a friend, Ruth Paine, but when Lee found work, she joined him in New Orleans. Marina later told reporters that Lee, driven by depression and paranoia, forbade her to wear lipstick, to speak English, and to smoke. He beat her on occasion and barked orders like a dictator. She had often thought of leaving him, and once even went to stay a friend, but she felt sorry for him, and returned.

In September 1963, he was once again out of work, and Marina's friend Ruth drove to New Orleans to get her and her baby. During her absence, Oswald became the self-declared chairman of the New Orleans chapter of the Fair Play for Cuba Committee, a pro-Castro organization. He also got a card at the New Orleans public library, and checked out several books, including a book about Kennedy entitled *Portrait of a President,* another about the Berlin Wall, several about Soviet and Chinese Communism, and a book describing the assassination of Huey P. Long.

On September 26, he took a bus to Mexico City, where he applied at the Cuban consulate for a transit visa for Moscow via Havana. When he was told it would take twelve days, he left in anger. The next day, he went to the office of the Russian consul general, announced that he was a militant Communist, and asked for a visa for the Soviet Union. Again, he was told there would be a long delay.

On that same day, the White House announced that President Kennedy would soon visit Dallas. Oswald returned to Dallas on October 4. Days later, Marina heard there would soon be a job opening at the Dallas School Book Depository, a clearing house in Dallas for public school textbooks. Oswald applied for, and got, the job. He started October 15 as an order-filler, with free run of the seven-story building.

Marina had her second baby around this time, and stayed with her friend in nearby Irving. Oswald took a small $8-a-week room in Dallas, and visited his wife on weekends. From a Chicago mail order house, he bought a carbine with a four-power telescopic sight, which he hid in the Paines' garage.

On November 6, the White House disclosed Kennedy's Dallas date—November 22. On November 21, Oswald spent the night in Irving with his wife, a departure from his usual routine, and in the morning got a ride to work with a neighbor. Lee was carrying a package wrapped in brown paper, which he said contained curtain rods.

The famous Zapruder films, taken by an amateur photographer, showed what happened when the Kennedy limousine passed the Texas School Book Depository at 12:31 P.M. on November 22, 1963. The film runs approximately twenty seconds, recording a momentous event in the annals of American history. Although silent, it visually recorded the horror of those moments—a shot resounded, Kennedy clutched at his throat, Texas's governor John Connally slumped over, the second shot followed, and the third shot exploded in the president's head. The film was not seen by average citizens until it was entered into evidence as part of then-New Orleans' District Attorney Jim Garrison's case against Clay Shaw in 1969, and it was not seen by the general public until the mid-seventies.

WAS OSWALD A SOLE ASSASSIN?

The decision of the Warren Commission that Oswald was the sole assassin seemed to be the right one. The evidence of the hidden rifle with his palm prints on it, a rifle ordered from a mail order catalog of the same name that was on the literature Oswald had distributed, seemed damning proof. Other evidence of guilt was a map found in Oswald's room, which outlined Kennedy's motorcade route.

In addition, at the ambush window on the sixth floor of the Dallas School Book Depository, the building in which Oswald was working, were the remains of a chicken lunch, an empty coke bottle, and three ejected shells from the rifle bearing Oswald's palm print.

THEORIES OF A CONSPIRACY

But theories of a conspiracy abounded. Witnesses claimed to have heard shots from the "grassy knoll" in Dealey Plaza, along the route of the president's motorcade. The "single-bullet theory" suggested that a bullet traveling from the sixth floor window of the Book Depository could not have entered Kennedy's neck, exited his body, and struck Governor John Connally of Texas, who was seated directly in front of Kennedy. Another shot would have had to come from the grassy knoll area, in front of the limousine. But Oswald was dead, and could never confess to a conspiracy. This threw the spotlight on Ruby, who was given a life sentence—but he wasn't talking.

Questions arose as to whether Kennedy was killed by a bullet that hit him from the front. This would certainly indicate a conspiracy. Articles and books flooded the media, giving readers food for thought about the "mysterious deaths" of many possible conspirators, deaths that in the clear light of day were not so mysterious at all.

District Attorney Jim Garrison "had evidence of a conspiracy" in the assassination of President Kennedy. (Courtesy Times Picayune *Publishing Company)*

Clay Shaw, New Orleans businessman, was indicted by Garrison on charges of conspiracy to assassinate JFK. (Courtesy Times Picayune *Publishing Company)*

New Orleans' flamboyant district attorney Jim Garrison proposed a series of theories, most of which the press called "bizarre." At first he called the conspiracy a "homosexual thrill killing" but as time went on, and conspiracy buffs flocked to New Orleans, it evolved into a massive CIA, FBI, and federal government plot. With Garrison's so-called evidence, he arrested retired businessman Clay Shaw on charges of conspiracy to assassinate the president.

A former World War II major, Shaw had become executive director of the International Trade Mart. He had been a prime mover in restoring the French Quarter, where he lived. But Garrison put together a trial based on hearsay and conjecture. In a *Playboy* interview, he listed the sinister cast of characters he believed were in Dealey Plaza the day of the assassination.

GARRISON'S WITNESSES

For two years, from 1967-1969, Garrison called one sleazy, eccentric character after another to the stand. His key witness was Perry Raymond Russo, who told the story of an "assassination party" in which Shaw, David Ferrie, and Lee Harvey Oswald discussed killing Kennedy. Yet Russo's story underwent a remarkable evolution between the time he came forward and the time he gave his court testimony.

In the end, the jury acquitted Shaw in less than an hour, citing a lack of evidence. The trial had ruined Clay Shaw's health and his life. He died in 1974.

THE HOLLYWOOD VERSION OF THE CONSPIRACY

Hollywood usually takes liberties with historical events, but in the movie *JFK*, director Oliver Stone turned the entire case upside down. Stone wanted to overturn the verdict in the Clay Shaw trial. The jury found that the district attorney had no case, so Stone invented one on film. Kevin Costner, playing Jim Garrison, argued the case in court and gave what Stone considered a memorable closing argument. Garrison had not tried the case himself. The movie was an Oliver Stone fairy tale. And talk about type casting! Little 5' 7" Kevin Costner was a curious Jim Garrison, who measured 6' 6" in his stocking feet.

WAR AMONG THE CONSPIRACY BUFFS

The conspiracy believers were split in their attitude toward Garrison. Authors Tony Summers, Henry Hurt, and David Lifton thought he was reckless and irresponsible. Yet he had many supporters among the conspiracy buffs. Here is David Lifton's view of Garrison:

> "I think it's ugly when the power of the state is arrayed against an innocent man—and the witch hunt that took place in New Orleans in 1967-1969 will always remain that: an ugly incident in the annals of jurisprudence."

Rosemary James, a local reporter, stated in an article for *Newsweek*:

> "He went from a highly intelligent eccentric to a lunatic in the period of one year. Every time press interest in the case would start to wane, he would propound a new theory. One week it would be 14 Cubans shooting from storm drains. Another week it would be H. L. Hunt and the far right in Dallas. This was no Robin Hood—no Untouchable either." *Newsweek, 12/23/91*

25

THE GARRISON CASE, CLOSE TO HOME

During the long and tedious years of newspaper and television reports of the trial, Garrison and his family lived directly across the street from us in Bancroft Park. *Perhaps he had received death threats*, we thought, when we saw security guards showing up in shifts, sitting before his door, day and night, armed with revolvers. No doubt they were there to protect his children. But our own children were often there, and those of our neighbors. And if his children were targets, then so were ours. That armed guard instilled fear in us all. With the exception of Clay Shaw himself, no one was more relieved when the trial ended than the residents of Bancroft Park.

CHAPTER TWO

Not "Black" Schools,
Not "White" Schools,
Just Schools

"The clock has ticked its last tick for tokenism and delay in the name of deliberate
speed."
                                                    Judge John Minor Wisdom,
                            U.S. Court of Appeals for the Fifth Circuit.

AS FAR BACK AS 1956, a three-judge United States District Court in New
Orleans, consisting of J. Skelly Wright, Herbert W. Christenberry, and John
Minor Wisdom, had ruled that segregation in public schools was illegal under the
Brown v. Board of Education of Topeka decision of 1954. Federal District Judge
J. Skelly Wright (Bush v. Orleans Parish School Board, 1956) then ordered the
school board to " . . . make arrangements for admission of children . . . in a racially
non-discriminatory basis with all deliberate speed."

MAYOR SILENT ON THE SUBJECT OF INTEGRATION

By June 1960, the school board had still done nothing to implement the order.
Neither had they been pressured to do so by Mayor deLesseps S. Morrison, who
refused to take sides in the controversy. He was convinced that his best strategy
on the subject of integration was neutrality.

In April 1960, Morrison refused the use of the publicly owned Municipal
Auditorium to Thurgood Marshall, director-counsel of the Legal Defense and
Education Fund, Inc. of the National Association for the Advancement of
Colored People (NAACP). "I thought their use of the facility would promote
controversy," he said.

Governor Jimmie Davis, as well as Attorney General Jack Gremillion and
members of the state legislature, had all been vocal in their opposition to integration of the schools. But the mayor and businessmen of New Orleans were
totally silent on the matter.

THE MOVE TOWARD SCHOOL INTEGRATION

In 1959, the NAACP asked Judge Wright to order the school board to provide a definite plan for desegregation. In July 1959, Judge Wright ordered the public schools to begin desegregation with the first grade in September 1960. The operative move toward school desegregation had begun.

AN APPEAL TO THE GOVERNOR TO INTERPOSE HIS POWERS

The school board now appealed to Governor Davis to interpose his powers between the courts and the people of Louisiana. To this end, the Governor gave permission to the legislature to enact several laws that would prohibit the allocation of funds to integrated schools and would allow the governor to close all integrated schools to "prevent violence or disorder."

On July 25, 1960, Attorney General Jack Gremillion filed suit in state court to prevent the integration of Orleans Parish public schools. Four days later, Judge Wright granted a permanent injunction against the Orleans Parish School Board.

CITIZENS OPPOSE SCHOOL CLOSURE

In the newspapers each day, the public was warned of the dangers of school closure—the prospect of juvenile delinquency, the cost of private schools, the loss of federal funds, etc. Church groups backed the movement to keep the schools open, but Mayor Morrison maintained his silence. When, however, letters from citizens concerned over the closure of public schools grew to alarming numbers, Morrison asked the City Attorney to give him a legal ruling on his responsibility as mayor in the school situation. On August 10, 1960, the attorney stated that "neither the Mayor nor the City Council has any jurisdiction over the school board in connection with its facilities and operations."

This is what Morrison had been waiting to hear. It got him out of the arena and allowed him to throw the burden of decision making on the shoulders of Governor Davis. That same day, he wrote the governor. "The . . . effects of closed public schools could have a heavy impact on community well being." Then he asked the most important question. How did he (the governor) intend to keep the schools open and segregated?

GOVERNOR DAVIS TAKES OVER

Governor Davis was quick to answer. On August 17, 1960, he assumed control of the Orleans Parish public schools and named Dr. James Redmond, city superintendent of schools, as his agent. To the amazement of the state officials, thirty-one white parents asked the courts to temporarily prevent state interference with the operation of Orleans Parish schools and to void eighteen state segregation laws that constituted "an evasion scheme designed to nullify school desegregation orders."

On August 27, a three-judge panel issued a temporary restraining order against Governor Davis. Two days later, the court restored control of the Orleans Parish public schools to the school board, struck down several state segregation acts, and directed the New Orleans school board to obey the desegregation order.

SCHOOL BOARD BEGINS TO COMPLY

Compliance with the order was not easy to obtain, but the tree was beginning to bend. The four moderate members of the school board, including the leader,

Lloyd Rittiner, at last expressed their belief that the public schools could no longer operate on a segregated basis. The *Times-Picayune* and the *States-Item* ended their silence with editorials backing "open" schools. On August 30, the four school board members met with Judge Wright and told him they wished to comply with his orders, but they did not yet have a desegregation plan. They asked him for a stay in the desegregation plan and the judge extended the date until November 14, 1960. By this date, Negro students would have already registered in their own schools, the school board members reasoned, and they assumed that few black children would make the effort to transfer.

LUNCH COUNTER SIT IN

On September 9, 1960, seven members of the Congress on Racial Equality, five black and two white Tulane University students, staged a peaceful lunch counter sit-in in a downtown department store. Police arrested the seven for "disturbing the peace." This was the first organized lunch counter sit-in in New Orleans. Others followed, as well as peaceful picketing outside the retail stores. The mayor directed the police to stop these demonstrations, which were "not in the public interest of this community."

GOVERNOR CLOSES THE SCHOOLS; JUDGE WRIGHT ORDERS THEM INTEGRATED

On November 8, 1960, Governor Davis signed into law the legislative acts that permitted him to close state schools. On November 10, Judge Wright issued a restraining order preventing the interference of the state committee in the operations of Orleans Parish public schools. The legislature fired Dr. James Redmond as superintendent of schools and froze the assets of the Orleans Parish school board. Judge Wright ordered the integration of public schools to proceed.

FIRST FOUR BLACK CHILDREN TO INTEGRATE NEW ORLEANS PUBLIC SCHOOLS

On November 14, 1960, United States marshals escorted four black first-grade girls to two public schools. Ruby Bridges was taken to William Frantz School. Leona Tate, Tessie Prevost, and Gail Etienne were escorted to McDonogh 19. Both schools were in the lower ninth ward of the city.

The parents of the children in these two schools were poor working-class people, many of whom lived in housing projects. They believed that integration would further reduce their economic and social well being. In those neighborhoods, race relations were bad because Negroes had replaced white workers in their jobs by working for lower wages. These neighborhoods also received the smallest benefits from Morrison's improvement programs. In addition, the ninth ward bordered St. Bernard Parish, where segregationist Leander Perez frequently inflamed white parents with his comments.

White mothers in the neighborhoods, learning of the plan to integrate their schools, rushed to the schools and took their children out. Throughout November and December, they met the black children at the schools each morning with screams and obscenities and threats. They spat at them and threw rocks at them. City police protected the children, but allowed the women to gather at the schools and did not arrest them for disturbing the peace, as they had arrested the blacks and whites who sat in at the lunch counter.

On November 14, 1960, Ruby Bridges, one of the first four black children to integrate the white schools of New Orleans, entered William Frantz School in the lower ninth ward with her mother and four U.S. marshals. (*Courtesy* Times Picayune *Publishing Company*)

(Courtesy Times Picayune *Publishing Company)*

THE SHAME OF NEW ORLEANS

This episode, covered by national news media, was called "The Shame of New Orleans."

The father of Ruby Bridges was fired from his job when his daughter began to attend the formerly all-white William Frantz School. White parents, who allowed their children to remain in the school where Ruby was, also lost their jobs.

DEMONSTRATIONS AGAINST INTEGRATION

On November 15, 1960, at the Municipal Auditorium, Citizens' Council leaders Leander Perez and State Senator William Rainach addressed a crowd of 5,000, ordering them to demonstrate against the NAACP, the Communists, the Zionist Jews, Judge Wright, and "that weasel, snake-head mayor of yours." The following day, a mob of 3,000 teenagers marched on the Civic Center Complex, shouting, "Two, four, six, eight, we don't want to integrate." Some marched into City Hall, demanding to see the mayor. When the mob turned toward the Board of Education Building at 703 Carondelet Street, mounted police and motorcycle officers stopped them and firemen used hoses to disperse them. The teenagers broke up into groups and walked in and out of the business district, throwing bottles and cans at buses and cars carrying black people. Several teenagers were arrested.

That night, Negroes took to the streets. Superintendent of Police Giarrusso reported the arrest of 250 people charged with loitering and carrying concealed weapons. On television, Mayor Morrison urged parents to keep their children in school. He said the police were not there to enforce orders related to school integration, but only to maintain law and order.

On November 28, when public schools reopened after Thanksgiving, the mothers returned and an angry mob followed Mrs. Daisy Gabrielle and her little daughter (another black student to integrate), shouting obscenities and smashing windows in the Gabrielle house. In December, the Gabrielle family surrendered

Civil Rights "sit-in" at the lunch counter in Woolworth's, 1960. (The Marion Jones Porter Collection, Courtesy Eric Waters and New Orleans Public Library)

to abuse. The father, James Gabrielle, quit his job and moved his family to Centerdale, Rhode Island, his place of birth.

A LULL IN THE WAR ZONE

In December 1960, there was a lull in the demonstrations at the two integrated schools. In March 1961, the United States Supreme Court upheld lower court decisions that nullified Louisiana's segregation laws. Organizations of Catholic men and women helped to promote interracial justice.

CHANGES IN RACIAL TOLERANCE

When Mayor Victor H. Schiro assumed office in 1961, he was immediately confronted with the problem of school integration, which was far from solved. The episode of the previous fall, with bystanders abusing the black children who broke the segregation barrier, was fresh in everyone's memory, and Schiro was determined to prevent such an incident in 1961. He instructed the police to set up barricades far from the school to keep die-hard segregationists away from the black children. Thus he avoided demonstrations and school integration proceeded more smoothly.

LANDMARK DECISIONS OF 1965-1967

But the fact was that, in 1965, eleven years after the Brown decision, less than one percent of the black children in Louisiana, Mississippi, and Alabama were attending schools with whites. Various school plans had been formulated that seemed to conform with Brown, but actually circumvented it. It was not until four landmark decisions were written by Judge John Minor Wisdom between 1965 and 1967 that the law on school integration was dramatically altered.

ENDS ACHIEVED BY AFFIRMATIVE ACTION

These decisions brought about the end of school segregation in the South because they required affirmative action on the part of public officials to integrate. In the last two of these cases, called Jefferson I and Jefferson II, Wisdom spelled out the law in detail, down to forms, letters, and practices to be used, telling exactly how school boards were to achieve integration. These cases are regarded as the most important of Wisdom's career.

In Jefferson I, Wisdom wrote, "The only desegregation plan . . . is one that works." He said that an education system is one that included " . . . not white schools or Negro schools—just schools." He added, "The clock has ticked its last tick for tokenism and delay in the name of 'deliberate speed.'"

On March 29, 1962, the parochial schools of New Orleans were ordered to desegregate.

CIVIL RIGHTS ACT OF 1964

The Civil Rights Act, signed by President Lyndon B. Johnson in 1964 is a United States law that bans discrimination because of a person's color, race, national origin, religion, or sex. It primarily protects the rights of blacks and other minorities to seek employment, to vote, and to use hotels, restaurants, and other public places. The act authorizes the Department of Education to direct school desegregation programs in areas specified by the government.

CHAPTER THREE

One Giant Leap for Mankind

"The United States should commit itself to landing a man on the moon and returning him safely to the earth." [before the 1960s ended]

President John F. Kennedy, 1961, address to Congress

"The Eagle has landed."   Neil Armstrong, first man on the moon, 1969

I WAS TEACHING CIVICS and Current Events to ninth grade girls at St. Joseph's Academy when the Mercury program made its first manned flight. In the early sixties, the subject of space exploration fascinated students. What was space? Where did it begin? What was the earth's magnetic field? What was interplanetary space? A whole new field of scientific data was opening up to students of all ages. It was hard for teachers to keep ahead of their pupils.

THE FIRST MANNED FLIGHT INTO SPACE

I brought my television set to class on May 5, 1961, the day Alan B. Shepard, Jr., made the first U.S. manned flight into space. Aware of the importance of this history-making event, we watched in awed silence as the rocket's first-stage engines ignited and the vehicle lifted off the launch pad. As the announcer explained what was happening, we saw the first stage of the rocket fall away and the second stage begin to fire. Then it, too, fell away. The velocity for escape from the earth's gravity, called "3g," had been achieved. Then, after a fifteen-minute mission, Shepard began his return to earth by decreasing the spacecraft's speed and re-directing its path. Breathless, we absorbed every stage of the mission and applauded the spacecraft's return.

THE SPACE RACE

Every day I came to class with newspaper clippings and magazine articles about

This Saturn V rocket booster was the first to be built by the Boeing Company at the National Aeronautics and Space Administration's Michoud Assembly Facility. It was 33-feet in diameter. This first stage was 138 feet tall. It was launched in late 1967. The three-stage Saturn V space vehicle, designed to launch manned flights to the moon, measured 365 feet in total height and weighed in excess of 6 million pounds at liftoff. (Courtesy Lockheed Martin Michoud Space Systems)

the Cold War between the U.S. and the Soviet Union, and the resulting Space Race. My students already knew that on October 4, 1957, the Soviet Union had stunned the world by sending the first artificial satellite, *Sputnik*, into orbit around the earth. They knew that a month after *Sputnik*, Russia launched *Sputnik II*, a satellite carrying a dog named Laika into space, proving that animals could survive the effects of microgravity. In 1959, Russia's space probe *Luna 2* became the first probe to hit the moon, and in the same year, their *Luna 3* photographed the far side of the moon. It seemed the Soviet Union was far ahead of the United States in the space race.

WE HAD SOME CATCHING UP TO DO

American leaders vowed to do whatever it took to catch up. In January 1958, the U.S. launched the satellite *Explorer I*. This was followed by *Vanguard I*, launched March 17, 1958. These were smaller than the Soviet satellites because the rockets used to carry the satellites were smaller. Bigger rockets would be needed for manned lunar flight, and both nations began major programs of rocket design and construction.

Then, with Alan Shepard's first American manned flight into space, the rest of the world had to sit up and recognize that our technology was equal or superior to that of the Russians. We could put a man into space. The subsequent flights proved it: Gus Grissom's suborbital flight, John Glenn's orbital flight, the Gemini program, and the Apollo program, which would put a man on the moon. America was back to stay, with open programs to be shared by all.

THE NATIONAL AERONAUTICS AND SPACE ADMINISTRATION

The ultimate success of the U.S. space programs depended on centralized planning. In 1958, a civilian space agency was formed, called the National Aeronautics and Space Administration (NASA). This organization helped forge agreement among competing interests, including military branches, universities, the aerospace industry, and politicians.

In 1961, the National Aeronautics and Space administration acquired the Michoud facility, in what is today New Orleans East, through a property transfer from the Department of Defense. The site was to serve as a final assembly facility for the design, development, and manufacture of large space launch vehicles requiring water transportation to launch sites.

MICHOUD'S HISTORY

My students loved the story about the land grant of the original 35,000-acre Michoud property deeded to the Louisiana soldier/statesman Antoine Michoud by the king of France in 1763. (Actually, France had secretly ceded Louisiana to Spain in 1762, and no longer owned the land, but many grants were made by France, innocently or not, while the cession remained secret). The land, some 15 minutes from downtown New Orleans, served as a source of timber for ships and a hunting ground for trappers and fur traders. Later, and for almost 100 years, the Michoud family ran a sugar plantation there.

With the outbreak of WW II in 1940, 1,000 acres of the Michoud Plantation were acquired by the Maritime Commission for the site of *Liberty Ship* construction. In 1942, a contract was issued for the construction of 1,200 plywood cargo planes at the Michoud facility. In 1943, the main production building, 43 acres under one roof, was completed and construction of aircraft began.

When the war ended, Michoud was closed and the building was placed in the inventory of the War Assets Administration. The New Orleans Dock Board acquired the tract through a lease/purchase agreement to serve as an industrial development complex. But with the coming of the Korean War, the Michoud site was reclaimed by the federal government for the construction of 12-cylinder, air-cooled engines for tanks. The facility closed once again in July 1953.

NEW ORLEANS' IMPORTANCE IN THE SPACE RACE

In 1961, NASA acquired the Michoud facility for the assembly of *Saturn* rocket boosters. New Orleans' importance in the space race reached new heights in 1964 and 1965 with the successful launching of the first three Saturn boosters assembled at the Michoud facility. Two Chrysler Corporation-built *Saturn I* first stages, combined with their second stages, were launched May 25, 1965 and July 30, 1965, marking the end of NASA's pioneering Saturn I program. In 1966, the first two-stage *Saturn IB* space vehicle, powered by a Chrysler-assembled booster, successfully launched an unmanned Apollo spacecraft some 5,000 miles down the Atlantic test range. It was the first test in space of the spacecraft that was designed to carry Americans to the moon.

At that point in our space development, the first Michoud-built *Saturn V* first-stage was scheduled to be launched the following year. Thirteen *Saturn V* boosters were to be built in New Orleans by Boeing. The NASA Michoud Assembly Facility received contracts from the U.S. Government to produce these boosters. This was called defense contracting in the aerospace forum. Michoud was a division of NASA's Marshall Space Flight Center, headquartered at Huntsville, Alabama.

In 1966, at its peak of production through contracts granted to Chrysler and Boeing, the total labor force at Michoud reached 11,500. In that year, more than 30,000 persons toured Michoud's Manufacturing Building.

THE SPACE MISSIONS

Throughout the sixties, we were bombarded by the media with heart-stopping news about the astronauts and the space programs: the Mercury missions, the Gemini missions (in which Edward H. White II, became the first American to walk in space), and the Apollo missions, which would include the mission to the moon. The race to the moon dominated the space race in the sixties.

PRESIDENT KENNEDY'S CHALLENGE

In his 1961 address to Congress, President Kennedy asked the United States to commit itself to " . . . landing a man on the moon and returning him safely to earth before the 1960s ended." Rocket scientists considered this a foolish and irresponsible commitment. The space program had many stages to work through, many programs to complete, many rockets and boosters to build, and unmanned flights to make before it could consider a manned lunar landing. It would take much longer than nine years. Yet the president had committed us, and every man would put his shoulder to the wheel and give it his best.

TRAGEDY STRIKES THE APOLLO MISSION

During a preflight test for *Apollo 1*, scheduled to be the first Apollo manned mission, to be launched February 21, 1967, astronauts Virgil Grissom, Edward White, and Roger Chaffee lost their lives when a fire swept through the command module. The nation mourned. Exhaustive investigation postponed any manned launch for nearly a year.

THE EAGLE LANDED AS WE CROSSED THE MEXICAN BORDER

In July 1969, my husband, Al, and I and our two teenage children were traveling by car to Mexico. Courage, right? In the blistering heat, with Bob Dylan singing "Mr. Tambourine Man" on my son's tape recorder all the way across the vast, dusty prairies of Texas? We stopped at Laredo, Texas, for customs inspection. The wait was endless, and the inspectors were in no hurry. We asked if there was news about *Apollo 11*, then in flight to the moon. No one knew anything about it. Most of the workers knew no English. They looked at us as if to ask, "Apollo Who?"

We got out of the car and stood in a metal roofed pavilion, frying in the heat until an inspector marked our bags with a chalk mark. We were hardly out of customs and across the border into Mexican Nueva Laredo when little boys were all over our car like mosquitoes trying to wipe our windshield with dirty rags and vendors were trying to sell us straw hats. Then we heard static on our car radio signaling a coming announcement.

A VOICE FROM THE MOON

The next sound we heard was the voice of Neil Armstrong, talking to us via Telstar on our car radio. "Thirty-five thousand feet," he said. Then, "Twenty-five thousand . . . five hundred feet. Moon, you're looking beautiful. One hundred feet. Touchdown." We applauded as we rolled along the hot highway just outside Laredo at 3:19 P.M. Then Armstrong said, "The Eagle has landed." This was a moment in history. Through crackling static he added, "One small step for man . . . one giant leap for mankind." My skin prickled all over. I was glad our children were with us to share the moment. We had done it! We'd put a man on the moon before the sixties ended. President Kennedy had pushed us to it. By his commitment, he'd launched America on a voyage of endless discovery.

In Monterrey the next day, we were able to get a New Orleans newspaper to see the reaction of our hometown people to this unprecedented achievement. From Michoud, there were messages of jubilation and plans for future landings. Mayor Schiro was grinning at us broadly from page one, and from the candid photos taken by staff photographers, there must have been partying in New Orleans on the night of July 20, 1969. We were sorry, in a way, that we weren't there to share the excitement with our friends.

"One small step for man . . ."

CHAPTER FOUR

Vatican II— Changing Habits

As a teacher in a Catholic school in the sixties, I had a front row seat at the changes made by Vatican II, which affected my life from every direction. The liturgy of the Catholic Church, the curriculum in the schools, the make-up of the faculty, and the apparel of the teaching nuns—these were changing all around me.

VATICAN II, THE 21st ECUMENICAL COUNCIL OF THE CATHOLIC CHURCH

In Rome, in the years 1962-1965, the 21st Ecumenical Council, called by Pope John XXIII, was making universal changes symbolizing its openness to the modern world. After Pope John's death in 1963, Pope Paul VI continued the meetings, held in the fall of the four consecutive years. Changes were made in modern communications media, relations between Christians and Jews, religious freedom, the role of the laity in the church, and liturgical worship.

In New Orleans, the changes caused an uproar. The mass was now to be said in English instead of Latin, and the priest saying the mass would face the congregation instead of looking away from it. The loss of the Latin mass was so upsetting to many die-hard traditionalists that the pastor of St. Patrick's Church asked the Archbishop to grant him the privilege of having a Latin mass on Sunday mornings, and permission was granted.

Vatican II brought about changes in education in Catholic schools, the inclusion of the laity in the liturgy, and the relaxation of regulations for nuns, including a change of habit.

CHANGING OLD HABITS

The nun's habit had always been an institution of the church, recognizable all over the world, and over the centuries. Although each order had its own habit that varied from the others in minor ways, all consisted of a floor-length serge or cotton dress (of black, brown, or white), a head-dress of a flat or fluted bonnet,

Assembling for the last time in their old habits on Christmas Eve, 1967, are the Marianite sisters at Holy Angels Academy. The big change is about to take place, after midnight mass. (Courtesy Marianite sisters)

*In their comfortable new habits, the sisters attend a variety show at the
Academy. Left to right: Sr. Mary Dorothy, Mother Madeleine Sophie, Sr. Mary
Madeleine, and Mother Mary Cajetan. (Courtesy Marianite sisters)*

covering the forehead, ears, and usually the neck, and a hip-length veil. There was usually a belt, a rosary hanging from the belt, and a panel of cloth from neck to hem down the front. But in the sixties, the Pope issued a statement calling for nuns to come out of the "Middle Ages" and modify their habits.

It was a drastic change. In the case of the Marianite sisters, for example, the habit would henceforth be a shorter, jumper-like dress with a black blouse and a white dickey underneath. Their veils would be abbreviated, allowing the sisters' hair to show, which took a little getting used to by their students.

This was a half-way measure, which would eventually give way to simple street clothes, including a bit of makeup, if desired, and even hair color. But the decision for the first change was thrown open to the nuns themselves. They voted, and the vote was unanimous for the cooler, more comfortable attire. A few of the elderly nuns, though voting for freedom of choice, continued to wear the old habits.

The time designated for the official change for the Marianite Sisters at Holy Angels Academy was after midnight mass on Christmas Eve in 1967. The sisters attended mass in their old habits, then after mass, retired to change into the new, while their students waited anxiously for them to reappear.

When the sisters returned to the chapel, transformed by their "new look," the girls gasped in wonder. They pressed their hands to their cheeks and smiled trembling smiles, wondering how they would relate to their teachers in modern garb. At first, the sisters were strangers to them, but in a short time, they seemed even closer than before, and the girls felt it easier to talk to them.

Showing mixed reactions to the sisters' new habits are Academy seniors Elaine Gadonneix, Ann Conrad, and Adele Baltazar. (Courtesy Marianite sisters)

VATICAN II AFFECTS ALL CATHOLICS

Vatican II made changes that affected every Catholic in one way or another. Nuns were no longer restricted to teaching and nursing, but became religious coordinators in parishes and took positions in the public schools. They became directors of sacramental programs, assisting the priests in their many responsibilities. They supervised schools at the diocesan level and directed public health services. One sister became the television production manager for the U.S. Catholic Conference in Washington, D.C., another a medical doctor, another a medical technician, and another a medical records secretary. The sisters were free to choose these professions, but many, who had become nuns to lead a quiet life of "blind obedience," were confused and unhappy about this new freedom. The religious mystique was gone—they were being sent back out into the world again.

Some left the orders and others changed their minds about entering. For all these reasons, there were not enough sisters left to teach in the Catholic schools, and lay teachers became the backbone of the faculties.

Besides reciting the mass in English, everyone in the congregation was now turning to give his neighbor the handshake of peace before going to communion, an innovation that many resented as an invasion of private prayer. But the teenagers enjoyed many new privileges, such as being altar servers, readers, and musicians. Adults revered the privilege of distributing communion. It was a time of such drastic change, in everything from religion to fashion, that the parents of teens could only shake their heads as they glimpsed their daughters in guitar groups on the altar in their embarrassingly short skirts. The Pope had asked for change, drastic change. But did he have that in mind? We had to wonder.

The New Liturgy allowed participation of students in the mass. The guitar mass was popular with the teenagers. (Courtesy Marianite sisters)

CHAPTER FIVE

Hurricane Betsy and Other Horrendous Happenings

"Don't be afraid. Don't believe any false rumors unless you hear them from me."

Mayor Victor Schiro

ON THE NIGHT OF SEPTEMBER 9, 1965, Hurricane Betsy hit Grand Isle with 145-mph winds and 12-foot tides. Before midnight on September 9, and in the early-morning hours of September 10, it pounded New Orleans with the same fierce winds, rocking houses, sucking out windows, and knocking out power all over the city. In the south and east of the city, it broke levees, releasing 20-foot walls of water.

The Industrial Canal bridge in Orleans Parish gave way, and low-lying subdivisions like Carolyn Park in Arabi were hit the worst, flooding with up to 9 feet of water—in some cases, up to the roof lines of houses. A wall of water flattened low-lying villages in St. Bernard and Plaquemines. Seventy-five people were killed and 15,000 injured in Louisiana and Florida. Thousands were trapped in attics, on rooftops, and in boats on a vast lake that stretched from the Industrial Canal to the Gulf of Mexico.

EVERYONE LISTENS TO NASH

Those who were fighting for their lives or swimming to a place of safety didn't have the luxury of watching television for news of the hurricane's development. They were at its mercy. But we were among the lucky ones. In our home in Lakeview, Al and I and our children watched Nash Roberts, the trusted New Orleans weatherman, who was broadcasting remote from the Sheraton Charles, the old St. Charles Hotel. His make-do studio had a plate glass wall overlooking St. Charles Avenue. At the apex of the storm, heavy rocks broke the plate glass and a piece of glass hit the back of Nash's neck, but miraculously, he was not badly hurt. Two inches of water flooded the room, covering the many cables and shorting out everything. Everyone in the studio was afraid of being electrocuted.

47

Many hurricane Betsy victims (September 1965) taking refuge in shelters or with friends or relatives were evacuated in military amphibious vehicles and small craft. The parked cars in this picture weren't going anywhere, so families awaiting evacuation had to wait for the next evacuation boat. (Courtesy American Red Cross, photo by R. Vetter)

Opposite: As far as property loss, Betsy was the worst hurricane ever to hit the Gulf Coast of the United States. The Red Cross listed 2,600 homes destroyed, 164,000 damaged. Water in this area was almost above car tops. Imagine the mess in the homes. (Courtesy American Red Cross, photo by R. Vetter)

MAYOR SCHIRO WARNS AGAINST FALSE RUMORS

Meanwhile, at WDSU-TV, Channel 6, Alec Gifford invited Mayor Schiro to come to the station and make it his headquarters throughout the hurricane. Schiro and Police Chief Giarusso came, Schiro wearing his yellow slicker. Then the roof fell in, literally, and water poured in on them all. But they managed to go on with the broadcast. Later in the evening, Mayor Schiro made his famous malaprop. "Don't be afraid," he told the people of New Orleans. "Don't believe any false rumors unless you hear them from me."

OUR OWN EVACUATION FROM THE LAKEFRONT AREA

We weren't laughing at the time, though. We were wringing our hands and waiting for directions. At around 9:00 P.M., the mayor advised all residents of Lakeview and the lakefront subdivisions to evacuate to a place farther from the lake. "Let's get out," my husband said. "Let's go to your mother's house." That's when I really got scared. I thought he would want to ride it out to take care of his property, but no. Within ten minutes, we were in our car driving against terrifying winds, not knowing when a giant oak would be torn out at its roots and fall across the street or on the roof of our car. We arrived at our destination, the two-story shingled house on Orleans Avenue near City Park.

My sister and her husband and children were already there. Her 10-year-old son was walking around the darkened house with a candle and a big smile on his face. "Wow!" he said, "this is living!" He thought he was Tom Sawyer in the cave with Becky Thatcher having a great adventure. But the long, frightening night soon robbed him of that fantasy.

My mother and grandmother were seated like statues in the living room saying their rosaries. After a few minutes, my father realized that my aunt, who lived upstairs, might be in trouble. He ran up the outside stairs, battling the wind, and entered her house to find her exhausted from holding the French doors together, the doors that led from her living room to her front porch. The key did no good at all, and she knew that if she let the doors fly open and the 140 mile-per-hour winds came through, the entire back of the house might fall away. My father managed to secure the French doors with heavy furniture and ropes, and disaster was averted. Then he brought my aunt downstairs to join the rest of the family as we waited out the night, listening to the screaming of the hurricane, the pounding of the rain, and the creaking of the house. From time to time, we lit fresh candles or brought milk or cereal or sandwich makings from the kitchen. We had nothing hot. We had lost all power, all heat, all light.

SURVEYING THE DAMAGE

Dawn finally came and the winds subsided. Orleans Street was not flooded—it was on high ground, thank God. We returned home, taking detours around fallen trees, to find that our block was without lights and refrigeration and air-conditioning, and would remain so for more than a week. Our parkay floor had been under water and had to be replaced. It was buckled up like the humps on a camel. But that was minor compared to the losses so many had suffered.

When our telephone service was restored, I was finally able to find out how others had fared during the hurricane. The middle-aged woman who cleaned house for me twice a month had been on her way home when the winds became violent. She was on the St. Claude bus at the top of the Industrial Canal when

Loss of life during Hurricane Betsy was relatively small because residents heeded evacuation warnings. One thing is certain—Betsy surely fouled up this community by picking up large dwellings and hurling them about in a helter-skelter fashion. (Courtesy American Red Cross, photo by R. Vetter)

flooding on the St. Bernard side of the bridge made it impossible for the bus to descend. For hours, with the wind threatening to whip the bus and its occupants into the canal, the passengers, including Mattie, clung to their seats and prayed. In the morning they were rescued in Red Cross boats and taken to a shelter. Thank God, she survived the night and the danger.

My friend, Joan, had been changing her nine-month-old baby's diaper by candlelight when the baby fell from the bathinette. Her teenager sister caught her, but her leg was broken. With no telephone service, Joan could not reach the doctor. She had to take her baby, by candlelight, to the emergency room at Mercy Hospital and have them contact him. He met them there and called in a surgeon, who put a body cast on the infant and kept them overnight.

All the houses in the neighborhood of the Academy of the Holy Angels were flooded, and the sisters took in the homeless and made space for them in the school building on the second floor. They fed them and housed them until they could be taken to a shelter or to the home of a relative or friend. Mayor Schiro congratulated them on their heroism then and later, caring for victims of the hurricane at various shelters and hospitals. Other nuns did the same, I feel sure, but the work of the Marianites was of special interest to me since I had attended the academy and knew of the history of care the Marianites had always given the people of New Orleans in emergencies.

HURRICANE CAMILLE DOES AN ENCORE

Four years later, in 1969, Hurricane Camille glanced off New Orleans, leaving some fallen trees and broken wires, but did its greatest damage to the Mississippi Gulf Coast. Many New Orleanians had homes "across the lake," or spent time there on vacation or visiting friends, and considered Waveland, Bay St. Louis, Pass Christian, Gulfport, and Long Beach an extension of New Orleans.

The worst tragedy Camille left behind had to do with an apartment house on the waterfront in Pass Christian called the Richelieu. A group of young people living there decided to "ride out the storm" in the apartment house and have a "Hurricane Party." When the hurricane was over, only the building's foundation was left standing. Camille had blown the building and the partygoers to kingdom come.

SNOW FELL ON LOUISIANA

On New Year's Eve, 1963, the people of New Orleans saw snow flurries through their picture windows. One week earlier and we could have expected Santa to land on our rooftops. This was more a treat than a disaster, especially for our children, who had never seen snow before. It snowed for 18 hours, from New Year's Eve into New Year's Day, in thick memorable flurries. At a New Year's Eve party, our friends delighted in sharing stories about the kids having fun all day in the snow, making snowmen and having snowballs fights.

Snow fell on New Year's Eve, 1963, and New Year's Day, 1964. To the Central American boarders at Holy Angels Academy, who had never seen snow before, it was a miracle. (Courtesy Marianite sisters)

*Patrick and Anna Marie Mitchel (brother and sister) built a snowman outside City
Hall with the help of Mayor Schiro during the rare snowfall of January 1,1964.
(Courtesy Patrick Mitchel)*

WHITE KITCHEN RAZED BY FIRE

A real tragedy to New Orleanians was the destruction by fire of the White Kitchen restaurant, a Slidell landmark, built in 1936, where everyone from the Crescent City stopped for coffee and donuts on the way to the Gulf Coast. It happened in October 1962, shortly after it had been remodeled.

Fire destroyed the White Kitchen restaurant in October 1962. The Slidell land-mark, built in 1936, was a regular stop for New Orleanians on their way to the Gulf Coast. (Courtesy Times Picayune *Publishing Company)*

CHAPTER SIX

Reinventing
Poydras Street

WITH THE MOVEMENT OF THE POPULATION into the suburbs, city officials began to think of reconstructing the Central Business District in order to draw big business back to the heart of the city. Poydras Street, with its many small businesses and deteriorating buildings, seemed the ideal place to make this transformation. City officials believed that unless it was developed into a "New York" street, it would gradually become an economic graveyard.

THE OLD POYDRAS MARKET

The Poydras Market, which had stood for decades in a two-block island in the center of Poydras Street near Rampart, had served Faubourg St. Mary, just as the French Market had served the Vieux Carré. It had been torn down in the late thirties. No new construction had taken place on Poydras since then. Now was the time to widen and beautify the street in anticipation of major construction and heavy traffic.

SKYSCRAPERS GOING UP

Many new buildings were on the drawing boards—the Amoco Building, One Shell Square, PanAm—but every new skyscraper that went up meant something had to be torn down. The simple fact was that the old buildings had no more economic vitality. The new buildings would each give work to about 5,000 people, who would stay in New Orleans instead of moving elsewhere. Those 5,000 people would patronize the small shops and businesses that remained around them, like pressing shops, stationery stores, watch repair shops, and restaurants. It would revitalize an old slum area.

The Rivergate Convention Center, completed in 1968, anchored the river end of Poydras Street. It covered six city blocks and seated more than 16,000 people. Built by the architects Nathaniel Curtis, Jr. and Arthur Q. Davis, it was the best example of Expressionist Style architecture in the city and an ideal place for carnival balls. (Courtesy Arthur Q. Davis)

HOUSTONIZE NEW ORLEANS?

Almost every day, we read the term "Houstonizing" in the paper. Editorials argued that this was what the city needed, since apparently Houston was leading the pack economically. But New Orleans was old, and that was its charm. Nothing in Houston was old. If New Orleans tried to become Houston, it would lose its essence, its European culture, and its historical significance. For New Orleans, "Houstonizing" would mean the end of our tourist industry. This was a subject of controversy, but the tourist industry won out.

Nevertheless, bulldozers and cranes were brought into Poydras Street to create a 134-foot-wide boulevard for six lanes of traffic, including a 22-foot-wide neutral ground. The new Poydras Street, extending from Penn Street to Delta Street, would be a major thoroughfare in the Central Business District and the street leading to the new International Trade Mart Complex.

Skyscrapers went up along Poydras to blend with the older buildings in a beautiful "mix" of the old and the new. Before the decade was out, the Rivergate (more detail is given in the next chapter) anchored the river end of Poydras Street, and ground had been broken for the Superdome, which would anchor the other end.

OTHER MAJOR IMPROVEMENTS IN THE CITY

In 1965, the new Municipal and Traffic Courts Building, part of the $9-million Police Complex, on Broad and Tulane, went into operation. The new House of Detention and Central Lockup would soon be a part of the complex.

A new bridge across the Orleans Canal at Filmore Avenue extended Filmore into Lakeview, opening traffic on Filmore from Pontchartrain Boulevard in Lakeview to Franklin Avenue at LSUNO.

Governor McKeithen signed the land transfer of 100-acre Camp Leroy Johnson on the lakefront to LSUNO for future development in 1964. An artist's concept of the campus showing six buildings was drawn in 1959. By 1969, ten buildings had been constructed.

IMPROVEMENTS IN AUDUBON PARK AND CITY PARK

The City Council appropriated funds to extend the vista of Audubon Park by 40 acres, from the levee to the river, increasing the picnic and recreational space. The City Park Board received $1,240,000 for improvements that included resurfacing its quarter-mile track, resurfacing the two miles of roadway in the park, reforestation and beautification, and, under its long time golf pro Henry Thomas, a new 18-hole golf course (the North course) and a new club house. The clubhouse was dedicated in 1966 and opened in 1967. It is the home of the City Park Gulf Club.

LEVEE PROTECTION WORK

Beginning in May 1965, the New Orleans Levee Board completed millions of dollars in levee protection work, adding to the safety of vast sectors of the city. Included were the Dumaine-Toulouse levee, protecting the vital Port of New Orleans; the Hayne Boulevard levee, protecting the eastern flank of the city; the Donner Canal levee, protecting Algiers; the Orleans Canal levee, Michoud-South Point levee, the 17th Street Canal levee, the Lakefront inner levee, and bulkheads at West End and at Seabrook.

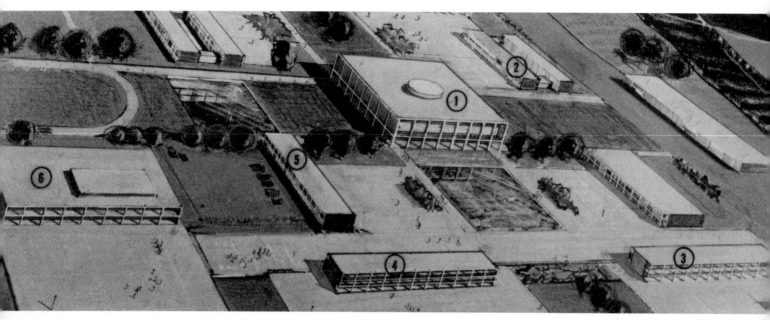

Artist's concept of LSUNO as it would look in 1966, viewed from the lakefront (drawn 1959). 1) Earl K. Long Library, 2) Science Building and Engineering Sciences Building, 3) Liberal Arts Building, 4) Education and Business Building, 5) Administration Building, 6) University Center. (Courtesy Earl K. Long Library Archives)

LSUNO buildings completed by September 1969, viewed from Leon C. Simon Blvd: 1) Liberal Arts Building, 2) Education and Business Building, 3) University Center, 4) Administration Building, 5) Earl K. Long Library, 6) Sciences Building, 7) Dining Hall, 8) Dormitory, 9) Central Utilities Plant, 10) Health & Physical Education Building. (Courtesy Earl K. Long Library Archives)

Funds were appropriated in the sixties for improvements in City Park that included a new 18-hole golf course and a new clubhouse. It opened in 1967. This recent photo shows it as it is now—the home of the Bayou Oaks Golf Club.

THE INTERNATIONAL TRADE MART

In 1965, the first tenant moved into the International Trade Mart, now called the World Trade Center, which rose 33 stories above the river. There would have been more tenants if Hurricane Betsy had not inflicted a quarter of a million dollars of damage. A beacon to world trade, this extraordinary building, topped with a revolving roof-top restaurant, was part of a world trade complex including a Spanish Plaza and the Rivergate, a $13.5 million International Exhibition Facility, under construction in the sixties.

Gov. John McKeithen signs the land transfer in 1964 of 100-acre Camp Leroy Johnson on the lakefront to LSUNO for future development. To his right, Hon. Milton E. Dupuy. To his left, first chancellor of LSUNO Homer L. Hitt. (Courtesy Earl K. Long Library Archives)

CHAPTER SEVEN

Activity on the Riverfront

THE RIVERGATE CONVENTION CENTER, completed in 1968, helped spur the development of Poydras Street as a major business artery. Built by the Board of Commissioners of the Port of New Orleans (Dock Board), it became, overnight, one of the city's most interesting sights. The Convention Center covered six blocks and provided 132,500 square feet of column-free exhibit space, making it one of the largest halls in the nation. It seated more than 16,000 people, or could hold up to 733 10'x10' booths. Two levels of underground parking provided space for 800 automobiles. The exhibit area was as streamlined and well-equipped as any in the world.

The architects of the Rivergate, Nathaniel Curtis, Jr. and Arthur Q. Davis, considered it the finest building they'd ever designed. With its free-flowing roof, it was the best example of the Expressionist Style of architecture in the city. This was the opinion of the late well-respected architect Sam Wilson.

SIZE OF THE RIVERGATE

The Rivergate was large enough for the giant floats of the new Mardi Gras Super Krewes to roll through with no problem whatsoever, making it an ideal location for carnival balls. It stood at the riverfront end of Poydras Street, with its line-up of beautiful new buildings going up almost as one watched.

The first time I saw the interior of the Rivergate, I gaped with absolute disbelief at the size of its interior. The event we were attending was the very first Bacchus Ball in 1969, with Danny Kaye as Bacchus. The parade's gargantuan floats were awesome. The enormity of the floats that rolled in and formed a circle around the dance floor, the bandstand, and the tables for ten brought into perspective the enormity of the building.

October 1961—view of the foot of Canal Street along the Mississippi riverfront from Poydras Street to St. Louis Street. The S.S. President is docked at Canal Street and the Canal Street ferry is at the landing. Many buildings of the Central Business District will be replaced in the sixties—the Dock Board building (behind garden area) will make way for the ITM Building. Behind that, space has already been cleared for the Rivergate Building. (Courtesy Historic New Orleans Collection, Museum/Research Center, Acc. No. 1984.166.2.143)

THE RIVERFRONT EXPRESSWAY

Sketches of a proposed Riverfront Expressway had been on the drawing boards since the forties. It was not to be just a short roadway, but a loop that would link New Orleans to the rest of the nation by connecting the city at both ends into interstate highways, thus tying New Orleans to the nation's major cities.

To some local officials, the sixties seemed an ideal time for its construction. The federal government was willing to pay 90 percent of the cost. What did it matter if it blocked the view of the river? It wasn't as if the residents of New Orleans were accustomed to having a river view anyway. For a century, sheds and warehouses had blocked their view of the river.

Throughout the sixties, the construction of the expressway raised heated arguments. It was an emotional issue that broke up businesses, law firms, and even families. The expressway, if constructed, would be an elevated highway, six lanes wide, 40 feet in the air, where 70,000 vehicles would pass each day. Drawings show it sweeping across the French Quarter, blocking the view of the Cathedral, the Cabildo, and the Presbytère from the river. The on and off ramps were to be at Iberville and Bienville, the narrowest streets in the Quarter. The expressway would then enter a tunnel under the proposed (but not yet built) Rivergate and emerge at Poydras Street, where it could tie in with the approach to the new Mississippi River Bridge.

TUNNEL BENEATH THE RIVERGATE

Federal funds for the tunnel had not yet been approved when plans for the Rivergate were ready. The disputed expressway and its tunnel were holding up the construction of the Rivergate. So the city of New Orleans wound up paying a million dollars for the tunnel, building it, and building the Rivergate over it. And then the tunnel was never used.

When the Rivergate was under construction, the elevated expressway was not yet a *fait accompli*. Opponents continued to point out that it would totally change the essence of the city and the mystique of the French Quarter. Preservationists like Martha Robinson got on the phone and talked to Representatives and Senators all over the country in opposition to the project. With William Long, owner of the *Vieux Carré Courier*, architect Mark Lowrey, Phil Johnson (who offered a nightly editorial on WWL's news program), WDSU, and the Clarion newspaper, she launched an extensive campaign to "Stop the Highwaymen."

But the proposal had the backing of the governor, state legislators, senators and congressmen, the mayor, and the *Times-Picayune*. How could it lose?

SAVE THE DEATH OF THE CITY

At Mardi Gras in 1966, opponents draped the balconies of the French Quarter with black crepe and put up posters reading, "Save the Death of the City." Newspeople came to New Orleans, saw the signs, and the issue soon appeared in *Life* and *Time*.

In 1968, Richard Nixon was elected president. After taking office in 1969, he appointed John Volpe Secretary of Transportation. Within days, headlines in New Orleans newspapers read, "Highway Defeated by Volpe. Riverfront Expressway Canceled." And the federal funds were diverted to another project. Its opponents were dancing in the streets. The proposed project was the first of its kind in the country to be canceled for historic preservation and environmental considerations.

July 1966—view centers on the site of the Rivergate Convention Center (under construction) and the new International Trade Mart. The area covered extends from Canal Street to Poydras Street and from the Mississippi River to South Peters Street. (Courtesy New Orleans Historic Collection, Museum/Research Center, Acc. No. 1984. 166. 2. 425)

THE PORT OF NEW ORLEANS

In the sixties, the Port of New Orleans was second only to New York in the value of foreign commerce and total waterborne tonnage. For two centuries it had been one of the world's major ports. Traffic continued to increase each year. A modern complex, Centroport, U.S.A., was underway, which would insure New Orleans its leading position for years to come.

The Dock Board operated the port. This five-man board of community leaders acted as landlord for the port, making wharves and facilities available by lease or rental, and implemented plans for future development. The Dock Board's home was a handsome two-story building at the foot of Canal Street, which was demolished in the sixties to make way for the International Trade Mart.

January 1959—the view of the Mississippi River Bridge as seen from the west bank of the river. The levee at Gretna is clearly shown. (Courtesy Historic New Orleans Collection, Museum/Research Center, Acc. No. 1984.166.2.112)

THE PORT, LOUISIANA'S LEADING INDUSTRY

The Port of New Orleans was Louisiana's leading industry, handling 80 percent of the state's exported manufactured goods and 50 percent of its agricultural products. It engendered an income of over $1.5 billion per year on the economy of New Orleans in the sixties. To insure its place as a leading industry, the Dock Board was compelled to conceive of a new plan of carrying the ever-increasing tonnage of exports in a more organized system.

Artist's concept of the proposed Riverfront Expressway (right), across Decatur Street from Jackson Square (left). At far end of Decatur we see the Café du Monde. The elevated expressway would have cut off the view of the Cathedral, Cabildo, and the Presbytère from the river. The proposal was defeated in 1969. (Courtesy Bill Borah)

THE MISSISSIPPI GULF OUTLET

In addition to South Pass and Southwest Pass, the port of New Orleans gained another and shorter route to the sea when the Mississippi River Gulf Outlet was opened to navigation in 1963. This channel ran 76 miles from New Orleans to the Gulf of Mexico. That made it 40 miles shorter than the Mississippi River route and free from many of the hazards of river navigation. In addition, it gave the Crescent City room for much needed expansion for industrial development.

Signs appeared in the French Quarter, like this one on the Napoleon House, demanding that plans for the expressway be stopped. (Courtesy Bill Borah)

THE CONTAINER REVOLUTION

The Port of New Orleans discovered that, despite its preeminence, it could easily lose cargo to other ports. The banana trade came to an end in the late sixties when the two big importers, Standard Fruit and United Fruit, left for Gulfport, Mississippi. The reasons were many. New Orleans' aging and cramped docks paled in comparison to Gulfport's state-of-the-art banana terminal. Another challenge for New Orleans would be joining the container revolution instead of being swept aside by it. Metal containers along the waterfront began appearing in the late sixties. They were, in fact, put into use as part of the Vietnam War effort.

Containers could be transferred directly from trucks to trains to ships with far less labor than conventional breakbulk cargo. Containers didn't require sheds; in fact, they needed lots of open space. So the Dock Board created a container ship terminal at the intersection of the Industrial Canal and the Mississippi River Gulf Outlet.

CENTROPORT, U.S.A.

In 1969, the Dock Board announced its 30-year port development plan, called CENTROPORT, U.S.A., patterned after Rotterdam's EUROPORT. It proposed building container operations along the Industrial Canal and gradually phasing out many older wharves along the riverfront. Ships, docks, and warehouses would all be changed to accommodate this new method of shipping over a 30-year period, ending in the year 2000.

Docks at the foot of Canal Street began moving in the direction of New Orleans East, where all docks would be lined up. There, containers of many sizes would hold a great deal more merchandise in far less space. This plan would clear the riverfront at the foot of Canal Street and Poydras Street for beautification and tourist projects such as the Aquarium, the World's Fair, the Moonwalk, and the Riverwalk.

The new facility would be known as the France Road Terminal, located on the west side of the Industrial Canal, near its junction with the Mississippi River-Gulf Outlet. It would be served by the Public Belt Railroad and would be accessible from two major highways.

Not all plans work out as conceived—not even day-to-day plans, let alone 30-year plans. In the past three decades, the plan has suffered many detours, but that will be for some other nostalgia writer to tell you about in the new millennium. In the sixties, however, this was the plan.

NEW TERMINAL ON THE SITE OF THE OLD DELTA SHIPYARD

A major portion of the new terminal was to be on the site of the old Delta Shipyard, where Liberty Ships were built during World War II. The facility would serve full-containerized vessels or vessels with mixed loads of containers and bulk cargo. Some 280 acres of land were available for the project, which would ultimately provide nine container berths.

In the Port of New Orleans in the middle sixties, there were active and growing container movements to and from the United Kingdom, continental Europe, the Mediterranean, Central and South America, Australia, the Far East, and the Caribbean. New Orleans was a thriving port city in a thriving economy.

CHAPTER EIGHT

Lakeside Mall, a New Way of Shopping

WHEN THOUSANDS OF VETERANS came home from World War II in 1945, they were facing unemployment, crowded colleges, housing shortages, the marriage boom, the baby boom, and the construction boom. No new houses or apartments had been built in the past fifteen years. Government loans for houses were available for veterans (GI loans, they were called), but these were only for the purchase of homes, not for renting. This prompted contractors to build thousands of low-cost houses in the suburbs on speculation.

These houses were quickly purchased, especially since many could be had with little or no down payment on the GI Bill. The suburbs became populated in record time, and intrastate highways were built to reach them. It was inevitable that, in time, the inner city would be abandoned and would deteriorate.

VETERANS IN THE SUBURBS—WHO'S IN THE INNER CITY?

There was an enormous amount of housing bought and occupied by veterans and their families in the suburbs. This allowed them to live in the suburbs and work in the city. The exodus to the suburbs begged the question—who would be left in the inner city? Several echelons of society would always be there: the rich, who had mansions on St. Charles Avenue, the Garden District, and the Metairie Country Club area; the upper-middle classes, who could afford to renovate their property; and the poor who could not afford to move or renovate.

In the late fifties, the population of New Orleans had begun moving out along the Airline Highway in a haphazard fashion. To get more people to move into Jefferson Parish, officials and promoters laid out Veterans Highway, which ran from Pontchartrain Boulevard to the St. Charles Protection Levee. Moisant Airfield in Jefferson Parish expanded to become New Orleans International Airport in 1960. And by 1965 I-10 ran from New Orleans to Causeway Boulevard.

October 1965. Lakeside Shopping Center was nothing more than a few stores in the center of a huge asphalt parking lot. As yet, there was no common roof and few shoppers. The shopping center was at the intersection of Veterans Memorial Boulevard and North Causeway Boulevard. Following Causeway Boulevard, we come to the cloverleaf I-10 interchange. (Courtesy Historic New Orleans Collection, Museum/Research Center, Acc. No. 1984.166.2.368)

In 1940, the population of Jefferson Parish was 50,427. By 1950, it had doubled to 103,873. And by 1960, it had doubled once again to 207,301. Its growth was phenomenal, totally unlike the slow spread of population in the original city in the two previous centuries. This swift sprawl stamped the parish with a homogeneous appearance. Houses that went up quickly looked alike, and did not have that special European quality visitors expected in the Quarter, nor the similarity of the shotgun doubles built in the Irish Channel in the twenties, nor the Spanish Revival look of houses built in Gentilly Terrace and on Canal Boulevard in the thirties.

LAKE PONTCHARTRAIN CAUSEWAY

Promoters had funded the most ambitious project of all in 1956, the 24-mile-long Lake Pontchartrain Causeway, the longest bridge in the world, which opened up the ozone belt of St. Tammany Parish to New Orleanians who didn't mind the long commute. By 1966, the second span was finished, at a cost of $14.8 million. This bridge was part of the nation's 41,000 mile Interstate Highway System.

CAUSEWAY BOULEVARD, "MAIN STREET, EAST BANK JEFFERSON"

The street that approached the Causeway was, of course, Causeway Boulevard, which became Main Street, East Bank Jefferson. And on that main street, in 1960, Lakeside Shopping Center was set in the middle of a vast asphalt parking lot.

LAKESIDE MALL—A NEW WAY OF SHOPPING

Causeway Boulevard and the surrounding area eventually came to be known as "Fat City" (so-named after the snowball stand, Fat City Snowballs, which was named after a movie/novel of the early seventies), hyping the promise of the fat profits that were to be made there by shopkeepers, restaurateurs, camera centers, and opticians who were willing to take a chance and open a business "way out there." The mall was the key to the development of the area. It was set in a neighborhood of middle and upper-middle class people who were invited to shop in a whole new way.

In the beginning, New Orleanians resisted the shopping mall. The word "food-court" was not in their vocabulary. Teenagers still hung out at Pontchartrain Beach Amusement Park, at neighborhood drug stores, and in the early sixties, at Lincoln Beach. New Orleans was not a shopping mall kind of town. It was a traditional town. Avant-garde styles took a year or two to get from New York to New Orleans. Shopping in New Orleans meant getting dressed up, taking a streetcar to Canal Street, strolling in and out of beautiful stores, and having dinner at a restaurant like Holmes'. But Lakeside Mall was out to change all that.

NO CLOCKS IN THE MALL

The mall was climate controlled, security patrolled, designed with few clocks, and little chance for a glimpse at outside scenery. The idea was to forget time and the rest of the world. In the mall, you could visit with friends, see a movie, exercise, get a haircut, give blood, view an art exhibit, and, of course, shop for clothes, jewelry, toys, pup tents, books, and just about anything else the average shopper could possibly desire—there was something for everyone. Lakeside Shopping Mall, and others like it, became a gathering place for teenagers, a place to have lunch, a meeting place for civic groups and auctions. It opened up a whole new way of life to New Orleanians and the denizens of Metairie.

CHAPTER NINE

The Vietnam War and the Flower Children

In THE FIFTIES, Vietnam was a war-torn country bordered on the north by Red China. In 1960, the Communist party of North Vietnam began full-scale guerrilla warfare to take over South Vietnam. A reign of terror escalated, aimed at wiping out anti-Communist leadership in South Vietnam.

When President Eisenhower left office in 1961, the United States had sent only military advisors to train the South Vietnamese soldiers, but no combat troops.

PRESIDENT KENNEDY'S VIEW OF THE VIETNAM WAR

In September 1963, two months before President Kennedy was assassinated, he was interviewed by Walter Cronkite. In that interview he said, "It's their war. They are the ones who will have to win it or lose it." This was his signal to the nation. Things were beginning to go badly in Vietnam, and he was getting ready to withdraw. It was Cronkite's opinion that if Kennedy had lived, he would have gotten out of the whole thing before we committed our fighting troops to South Vietnam.

Think for a moment of the long-range effect of the bullet fired by the paranoid Lee Harvey Oswald. With Kennedy gone, we were soon plunged into a no-win war where 2.5 million Americans served and 58,000 died, where the home front was so bitterly divided that sons parted in anger from fathers, and brothers went in different directions, some to fight and die, others to wander the country in tribes, with no place to sleep, no food, no sanitary facilities, all in rebellion against the past generation for the state the world was in and the war that had resulted.

HOW WE BECAME EMBROILED

The rebels, the flag burnings, and the hippie cult accelerated as the United States became more and more involved in the Vietnam War. When did our

The Flower Children invaded New Orleans and settled in Jackson Square, cooking on manhole covers and sleeping in the open. They were a cause for concern to city officials. 1968. (Courtesy Michael P. Smith, photographer)

The Flower Children protested against the Vietnam War on Tulane Campus,
1968. (Courtesy Michael P. Smith, photographer)

involvement begin? On August 2, 1964, the Commodore of the destroyer USS *Maddox*, patrolling in international waters off the coast of North Vietnam, in the Gulf of Tonkin, reported a number of high speed North Vietnamese PT boats moving parallel to his ship and closing in on it. The *Maddox* received permission to open fire when the range was eight thousand yards. The *Maddox* did so, and the American fighting war against North Vietnam began.

On August 8, 1964, after President Johnson's address to Congress and to the nation, Congress resoundingly passed the Gulf of Tonkin Resolution, giving the president the right to commit military forces to Vietnam. The resolution had been prepared months before. After the Gulf of Tonkin, LBJ had it presented to Congress. He had always believed that Truman made his fatal error in not going to Congress before getting into the Korean War.

THE DREADED DOMINO EFFECT

Many feared that Communism would eventually spread over Southeast Asia, taking control of one country after another, unless stopped by a strong American presence there. Also, the year 1964 was an election year, and the Republican hawks, especially Goldwater, were demanding more action against the Communists. It seemed to Johnson and his advisors a good time to go ahead with a greater American commitment.

By 1966, U.S. combat troops were engaged on the ground and U.S. Air Force planes were in the air over South and North Vietnam. By 1967-1968, more than a half million soldiers were involved in the fighting. Unable to score decisive victories in Vietnam, we were losing hundreds a week, and we all wondered how much longer it could go on.

THE WAR IN OUR LIVING ROOMS

At night, we saw the war played out on television in our living room. How could we not be aware of what was happening day by day? We saw the jungles. We witnessed the bloody massacres. Young men of draft age in New Orleans and all over the United States were strongly divided on the issue of war. Some volunteered in the way of their fathers, veterans of World War II. Some accepted the draft resentfully, but they accepted it. But thousands rebelled against being sent into "a foreign and immoral war," in which they felt America had no part.

After the Tet Offensive, most Americans realized we would not win the war. We were unable to score decisive victories. Military men in Vietnam thought, "What are we doing here?" Young men at home, breaking family ties, left home, some to go to Canada to escape the draft, some to wander to other cities like San Francisco, where they became flower children, living in communes, burning their draft cards, smoking pot and taking the drug LSD.

Living in a state of rebellion, they asked themselves, "Where is it written in stone that I have to work from 9:00 to 5:00?" They got up in the morning and had no idea what the day would bring. They were looking for new ways to express their disgust with the state of the world.

Parents in their forties had a hard time understanding the mindset of the hippie crowd. All they saw was a band of unwashed, unemployed drifters, using drugs, having sex, wearing beards, and looking dirty. What would become of them? What would their future hold?

The flower children came to New Orleans in droves. They were drifters with backpacks and guitars and no visible means of support. They wore cut-off jeans and tie-dye shirts and bands around their foreheads. The men had Afro hair styles or waist length straight hair. The girls wore short, fringed shirts, many printed with Indian designs, or jeans with T-shirts. They, too, had long straight hair with Indian bands. Men and women alike wore necklaces, bracelets, and earrings.

Mike Stark, an "older" flower child, set up a service center for the young flower children. He stayed on when the others left and opened a "Love Shop" in the Quarter, where he sold shirts, records, and posters. (Courtesy Michael P. Smith, photographer)

They settled into Jackson Square and barbecued on Sewerage & Water Board manhole covers. They held a "Love-In" in Audubon Park. The police were on full alert, expecting the worst, but the worst didn't happen. It was a picnic, like an Earth Day, and they played guitars and sang. But on the Tulane campus, they demonstrated against the Vietnam War.

City officials were concerned about their presence. They needed food, after all, and a place to sleep and to relieve themselves, even if they were willing to go without baths. They were not criminals, but they would, in time, steal to buy food, if nothing else.

Mike Stark was a middle-aged flower child who looked like Santa Claus, except for the red hair and beard. He was a local icon. He came with the younger hippies and took care of them in the New Orleans Free Clinic, which he founded in the Quarter (and which the N.O.P.D. frequently tried to close down). He took them to Charity Hospital when they were beyond his help. A homosexual, he was also a founder of the local Gay and Lesbian Coalition. He stayed on after the others left and opened a love shop in the Quarter, where he sold tie-dye shirts, posters, records, and incense.

CONTEMPLATING THE OUTCOME OF THE VIETNAM WAR

The United States had to wind down its participation in the Vietnam conflict and spend many years contemplating the outcome of that disastrous war before its young rebels felt a part of their country again. It was decades before they and all the other citizens paid the honor due the Vietnam veterans instead of calling them baby-killers. The flower children had to mature another ten or fifteen years before they could look back on the sixties as an unreal time, and in perspective, weigh it against the stability of home and family and a productive life.

CHAPTER TEN

Music—Rock 'n Roll is Here to Stay

MUSIC WAS THE VOICE of the anti-war, anti-establishment youth movement of the sixties. It was the expression of their way of life, from the ear-splitting sounds of electric guitars to the bearded, bare-chested musicians, to the drug-induced highs for which the music set the stage. The haunting, psychedelic sounds created the mood for the commune style of living of the flower children and the hippies. Nice kids were intrigued by the whole image and wanted to be a part of it, although they were not druggies. But this is what parents worried about.

From mid-century on, the music that sold tickets and records and albums came from small groups of young musicians, playing guitars and keyboards and singing songs, most of which they wrote themselves. It was hard for us, the parents of teenagers, to accept Rock 'n Roll. To us, it sounded like a lot of screaming and electrically enhanced shrills and clashes. We warned our teens they'd be deaf for the rest of their lives. But there was no getting around it. Rock 'n Roll was here to stay.

GLENN MILLER WAS ANCIENT HISTORY

Oh, how we old people (in our thirties and forties) missed the lilting, sentimental ballads of World War II. We missed the sweet clarinet lead of the inimitable Glenn Miller Orchestra in songs like "Sunrise Serenade" and "String of Pearls." Jazzy tunes sung in close harmony were his stock in trade as well, like "Chattanooga Choo-Choo" and "In the Mood." Back in the forties, we'd danced as couples, holding each other close, losing ourselves in the romantic mood his arrangements evoked.

But Glenn Miller was gone, a casualty of war, and his style of music, as well as that of Artie Shaw, Jimmy and Tommy Dorsey, Benny Goodman, and Harry James, were ancient history to the rockers of the sixties. The ballads of Perry Como, Frank Sinatra, and Tony Bennett were gone, too, except for the continued support of the older crowd. Some of these bands and vocalists would later return to popularity. They would appeal to a whole new generation of young people who would think they'd discovered them. By the seventies and eighties, the teenagers of the sixties would have grown older and would be ready to inject a little schmaltz into their music menu.

But at the top of the charts in the fifties was Elvis with his sexy, eyes-closed-and-hips-revolving music ("Blue Suede Shoes"). And in the sixties, it was the sad, close-harmony ballads of The Beatles ("Yesterday"). The Beatles, hardly out of their teens themselves, with their soup-bowl haircuts, their short Eton jackets, and skinny-legged trousers, had taken the teenagers of America by storm. Their look, their style of music, everything about them was different and revolutionary. They were fodder for the youth revolution of the decade.

Elvis and The Beatles represented Rock 'n Roll, which had taken the spotlight from the Big Band Sound. It was the music of youth, and adults need not approve nor partake.

FRENZY AT THE CITY PARK STADIUM

On September 16, 1964, The Beatles of Liverpool, England, were brought to New Orleans by Herb Holiday of WWL Radio. At City Park Stadium they played and sang, while thousands of young girls screamed and cried and fainted dead away. Swarms of teenage girls rushed the stage and would have torn the clothes off the singers' backs if the police had not held them back. The Beatles, unlike groups to visit New Orleans later, came on stage, played twelve tunes, and rushed off. The whole performance lasted about a half-hour. Although the promoters of the show ended up losing money on the performance, The Beatles had put their stamp on New Orleans, and our youth said yes!

Frenzy at City Park when The Beatles played in concert. Girls screamed and fainted and had to be restrained by police. (Courtesy WWL-TV)

*The Beatles on concert stage in City Park Stadium. Their
style stamped Rock 'n Roll as the music teenagers lived by.
(Courtesy WWL-TV)*

CAN'T TELL THE NICE KIDS FROM THE BUMS

To partake of this Beatlemania in the Rock 'n Roll generation, it was absolutely
necessary to look the part. My son and his friends didn't wait five minutes after
graduating from high school, where the dress code and hair code were strict, to
start growing long thick sideburns, beards, and shoulder-length hair. We, the parents, hated it, but what were we to do? We tried to fight it, of course, but every
boy argued that he'd look like a nerd, the only one in his crowd with a businessman's haircut and a shave. Well, it *was* vacation, and we prayed that in three
months, they'd realize that grungy was not beautiful.

I was glad my son and two of his friends had planned to backpack their way
through Europe that summer. At least my friends wouldn't have to see him for a
couple of months. He had worked part-time and saved every cent of his trip
money, and we were proud of him for that. So they were off to distant places,
three young men with long hair, beards, and mustaches, in T-shirts and blue jeans
that rarely got washed, looking for *pensions* at $2 a night. God only knew what
kind of bums (real bums) might latch onto them, thinking they were druggies or
hippies. At least no one would rob them, thinking them to be rich boys. We were
grateful for that.

BUBBLE GUM MUSIC

In the early sixties, Rock 'n Roll could not be played on the radio. On FM-
Radio, you heard "Easy Listening" or "Bubble Gum Music" played by groups like
Paul Revere and the Raiders or Herman's Hermits. This was a more subdued ver-
sion of rock. There was a playsheet at the stations listing the songs allowed.

Mike Costello, owner and manager of WTIX-FM, told me that the best-known
Rock 'n Roll radio station in New Orleans in the sixties was WTIX-AM. It was
part of Storz Broadcasting Company, owned by Tod Storz. As far back as the early
fifties, Storz noticed that wherever there were jukeboxes, people played the same

40 songs, so he decided to play only those songs on his station, and he'd always be playing a hit. "That's where 'Top 40' came from," said Costello.

Joe Costello owned and ran WRNO-FM, which was later taken over by his brother Mike. They played music that was away from the mainstream of Top 40s music, such as the Grateful Dead, The Doors, Steppenwolf, The Beatles, and the Rolling Stones. WRNO was called an "AOR" (or "Album Oriented Radio") radio station. They played the longer (7 or 8 minutes) version of a recorded song, whereas the AM stations played an edited version (3 to 4 minutes).

The other rock FM station in town was WWOM-FM, which was free-form and featured a disc-jockey known as Brother Judas, otherwise known as John Larroquette from *Night Court* fame.

Lt. Governor James Noe, Sr., owned radio station WNOE, but he let his children run it. His daughter, Gay Noe McClendan managed it first, then his son, James Noe Jr. The radio battles began in the sixties. It was a "Radio War Zone" between WTIX, owned by Tod Storz, and WNOE, operated by the Lt. Governor's children. WTIX-FM was a re-creation of WTIX-AM, which was the Number 1 Rock 'n Roll station in New Orleans from the early fifties to the late seventies.

RHYTHM & BLUES CONTINUE IN POPULARITY

Throughout the sixties, Rhythm & Blues artists' popularity grew, for New Orleans jazz, played and sung primarily by black artists, was legendary, part of the culture of the city. Allen Toussaint, for example, was, by the sixties, a pianist, composer, singer, producer, and partner in SeaSaint Studios, a prosperous man and a genius at his craft. At twenty-two, he was in charge of Minit Records' musical direction. He knew all the artists—Ernie-K-Doe, Irma Thomas, Aaron Neville (Toussaint's first cousin), Benny Spellman.

Aaron Neville was a handsome singer whose falsetto powers were recognized quite early in his career. He was said to "look like a football player and sing like an angel." Irma Thomas was then a young vocalist with a nice smile who would be known for the next thirty years as the Soul Queen of New Orleans.

Every producer and manager was looking for a white man who sang like a black man. This is why Elvis had made it so big in the fifties. Another white man who filled the bill was Frankie Ford, born Frankie Guzzo in Gretna, across the river from New Orleans. He was in grade school when Cosimo Matassa opened the J&M recording studio in the Quarter. Approximately ten years later, Frankie walked in one day and was thrilled to see famous R&B artists he had only heard of, including Huey Smith, the famous pianist and arranger. Huey had written a song called "Sea Cruise," and Joe Caronna and Johnny Vincent, talent agents, wanted it for Frankie. He was good looking and he could sing like a black man. Huey wanted to sing it himself, but he finally relented. They changed Frankie's name from Guzzo to Ford. Frankie cut the song, and it lay around for several months, and then finally he heard it on the car radio on the Hoss Allen Show on WLAC Nashville. It was then passed around to Miami and Cleveland and, at last, one night, Frankie heard it on the Dick Clark Show. "Sea Cruise" was vintage New Orleans R&B and Frankie Ford was a star.

JAZZ ARTISTS

In the sixties, old black jazz musicians played nightly in Preservation Hall. This gave them a chance to go on playing instead of sitting home in retirement. Jazz never waned in popularity. It was a special treat to tourists to hear New Orleans

Jazz played by people like Sweet Emma, with the bells on her skullcap and garters, playing the piano with her long stiff fingers, and singing with her raspy voice. No one seemed to mind sitting on backless benches in a room with broken glass windows, all of which added to the atmosphere.

NEW ORLEANS' OWN NATIONALLY ACCLAIMED MUSICIANS

New Orleans' own jazz artists, Pete Fountain and Al Hirt, had, by the sixties, been adored by local fans and tourists for twenty years. But by 1960, they'd also achieved national acclaim. In their early struggling days, they'd played together at places in the French Quarter, and added to their income by exterminating

Singer Irma Thomas, "Soul Queen of New Orleans," 1964. (Courtesy Irma Thomas)

termites in the daytime. But by 1960, they were stars. Al Hirt played for JFK's inauguration. In 1964, he won a Grammy for his recording of "Java." And at every Saints game, his horn provided a cheerful note, sometimes the only cheerful note in the whole afternoon. And Pete, fresh off the Lawrence Welk Show in 1959, was recording albums that sold by the millions. He organized his own band and his own nightclub that he would hold on to for the rest of the century. He was appearing regularly on network television shows, which would in time include more than 58 performances on *The Tonight Show* and four command performances at the White House.

On October 18, 1961, Wynton Marsalis was born. He would grow up to become a New Orleans jazz musician, trumpeter, and combo leader, and would receive unprecedented popular acclaim by winning Grammy awards for both jazz and classical performances.

Ronnie Kole, pianist extraordinaire, was another musical icon in New Orleans by the sixties. In the eighties, when Pope John Paul II visited New Orleans, Ronnie Kole, Al Hirt, and Pete Fountain were invited to play selections at the Pope's mass on the UNO campus at the lakefront.

CHAPTER ELEVEN

Television, Radio, and Books

To appeal to the demands of the ever-expanding youth market, television producers and writers tried to create shows that copied the cynicism of youth toward the older generation's beliefs and institutions. But what they turned out instead was an endless number of shows filled with adolescent silliness.

The Beverly Hillbillies (CBS, 1962) received terrible reviews, but the viewers loved it. Sitcoms like *Petticoat Junction, Green Acres,* and *The Andy Griffith Show* followed, giving rise to the television nickname, "The Rube Tube."

Then came exercises in fantasy and escape—*The Flying Nun, I Dream of Jeannie, Bewitched.* And others that were meant to make the military look silly—*Hogan's Heroes, McHale's Navy.* And those that made the police (as part of the "Establishment") appear ridiculous—*Car 54, Where Are You?*

Some shows were socially significant. *I Spy* was the first to cast a black actor, Bill Cosby, as a lead, teaming him with Robert Culp in a secret agent series. By the decade's end, the demands of youth forced television producers to create a show about an ersatz rock group called *The Monkees.* And in 1968, Rowan and Martin's *Laugh-In* gave us all a chance to laugh at reality. It was television's silliest decade, but it was a great way to escape, and it has lived on in syndication.

DISASTER PLAYED OUT IN OUR LIVING ROOMS

There was a lot to escape from in the sixties. Television gave us front row seats at the world's disasters. We witnessed the killing of a president. We saw Bobby Kennedy lying in his own blood on a hotel floor moments after proclaiming victory in California's Democratic presidential primary election. We saw our young men dying in the swamps of Vietnam, riding in helicopters to pick up wounded soldiers in snake-infested jungles. It was too much, it was too close. We were more aware of the horrors of war than any human beings in the history of mankind, and more repelled by it. "Hey, hey, LBJ, how many babies did you kill today?" It sickened us all.

Every hurricane, every fire, and every heinous murder was right in our faces. They were more vivid than articles in the newspaper had ever been. We saw them happen, and we heard the screams.

LOCAL TELEVISION: NEW ORLEANS COULD BE PROUD

Television could be fun, too. After supper, at night, the family would get comfortable around the television and check out the evening fare. New Orleanians were justly proud of the success our local stations had attained by 1960. WDSU-TV Channel 6 (an NBC affiliate) first aired in 1948 with stars like Mel Leavitt, Terry Flettrich, and Nash Roberts. Mel could do it all and do it well. As sportscaster, newscaster, quiz show host, and author of prize-winning documentaries, Mel was the best known and best loved television personality in New Orleans.

In the sixties, WDSU-TV was at 520 Royal Street (the old Brulatour mansion). To the right, beneath the awnings, was Flo Salter Dolls, a popular tourist shop. To the left, an art shop and The Little Toy Soldier, where lead soldiers and other images were designed. To the far right, in the next block, the Wildlife and Fisheries Building is visible. (Courtesy Paul Yacich)

Mel Leavitt, WDSU-TV newscaster, invited Mayor deLesseps S. ("Chep")
Morrison to review the station's recent and previous achievement awards, 1960.
(Courtesy Paul Yacich)

Terry Flettrich was the First Lady of New Orleans television. Even before WDSU was officially launched, she was starring daily in 15-minute fashion and cooking shows produced at D. H. Holmes and shown live on television sets for sale in the store. When WDSU went on the air, she moved over to the station, but continued to pitch D. H. Holmes' department store. In her 25 years with WDSU, she was Mrs. Muffin, a children's show star, and hostess of *Midday*, a show that delivered information and fun.

Nash Roberts, soft-spoken weatherman, started at WDSU in 1949 and spent 50 years giving us information about the weather. He became our local hurricane guru, and even after retiring, showed up at WWL when a hurricane threatened.

Terry Flettrich, WDSU-TV, played Miss Muffin to the city's children for many years, including the sixties. (Courtesy Paul Yacich)

Another WDSU-TV pioneer was Paul Yacich, the engineer who put the first antenna atop the Hibernia Bank Building in 1948. A multi-talented behind-the-scenes worker, he became a writer, producer, and director of special projects. In 1999, Yacich was inducted into the Radio and Television Hall of Fame.

LOCAL ADDITIONS IN THE FIFTIES AND SIXTIES

Many new talents were hired in the fifties, and many of these were still around in the sixties: Bill Monroe, Alec Gifford, Al Shea, Wayne Mack, and others. WWL-TV signed on as a CBS affiliate in the fifties.

John Pela hosted the WWL-TV *Saturday Hop/The John Pela Show*, which ran from the fifties through the seventies. This weekly program showcased 30 couples, minimum age 14, maximum age seniors in high school. They did the Twist, the Frugue, the Swim, the Boogaloo, the Pony, the Popeye, and others. These dances had moves that were just a shade short of bumps and grinds, and Pela had a hard time trying to keep the show from looking like burlesque. Teenagers all over town waited for the program, studied the steps, and prayed they would someday be on the show.

Also big on WWL in the sixties was Morgus the Magnificent (Sid Noel), whose show, *The House of Shock*, started January 3, 1959, and ran through the sixties (despite a three-and-a-half-year absence when Morgus went to Detroit!). Morgus was the mad scientist who performed wacky experiments in the breaks between Frankenstein and Dracula movies.

When the sixties began, the popular Bob & Jan Carr were still on the radio, on WWL-AM, 870, interviewing celebrities and politicians having breakfast at the Roosevelt Hotel (now the Fairmont). In 1961, they moved over to WDSU-TV with a show called *Second Cup*. Then two years later, they moved again to *Midday* (WDSU-TV) with Terry Flettrich. After four decades of radio and television broadcasting, Bob and Jan are together again on radio in the early morning hours on WBYU Radio, swapping banter as couples do after 48 years of married life.

Phil Johnson spent 39 years as a WWL newsman, beginning in 1960, and presenting editorials nightly from 1962 until his retirement. Over the years, he served as promotions manager, editorialist, and news director, winning three prestigious Peabody Awards for his documentary work.

Don Westbrook, another 39-year on-air veteran at WWL-TV, was best known over the years for his weather reports. He, too, began in 1960.

Buddy Diliberto was the sportscaster who gave reports of the Saints' current defeats with a bag over his head, a symbol of sports-fan disgust, and began calling the team the "Aints."

Jerry Romig moved from sportswriting at the *States-Item* newspaper to WDSU-TV in 1955. During his twenty-year television career, he was a news reporter, editorialist, producer, and program director, overseeing the *Midday* show and collaborating with Mel Leavitt in the award-winning documentary, "Huey Long."

Dozens of other talented stars came to television before, during, and after the sixties, but are too numerous to mention in any great detail. For instance, Dick Van Dyke started at WDSU in the fifties, but by the sixties he had his own national sitcom. Jim Metcalf, a pioneer in local television and a national, best-selling poet in his lifetime, worked at WWL. And Hap Glaudi, the WWL sportscaster for thirty years, is credited with pioneering "Happy Talk" news, best associated with figures such as Willard Scott and Al Roker.

Every Saturday afternoon on the John Pela Show *on WWL-TV, teenagers of New Orleans danced to a Rock 'n Roll beat. (Courtesy John Pela)*

94

WATCH
"SATURDAY
HOP"

Bill Wilson of WWL-TV welcomes Ava Gabor to "Hollywood Premiere" at entrance to Antoine's Restaurant, where stars will celebrate the beginning of color movies on Channel 4. (Courtesy Bill Wilson)

The sixties were a struggling time for radio stations and personalities, who tried to hold on to listeners who were fleeing by the thousands to their television sets. What could radio do to stay alive? What could be heard on radio that could not be seen and heard on television?

First of all, as we have said, there was rock music and the place to hear it was WTIX, 690 on your dial, "The Mighty Six-Ninety" station. That pulled in the young listeners. Other Rock stations were WNOE, WRNO, and WYLD, a rhythm and blues station.

On WSMB-AM, 1350 on the dial, two men who became the best known radio talk show hosts in New Orleans, Roy Roberts (Roy Makofsky) and Jeff Hug, began being called by their radio nicknames, "Nut & Jeff." Initially, they played records and read news, sports, and weather. But they began to chat more and more, Roy laughing hilariously at Jeff's stories, and vice versa. People tuned in while having breakfast or getting dressed for work to start off their day with a hearty laugh at the antics of these two entertainers. Their popularity was such that when they hosted golf tournaments in the Bahamas or in Acapulco, they couldn't handle the numbers. Later (in the nineties) they were among the first inductees in the Greater New Orleans Broadcasting Hall of Fame, along with Larry McKinley, former WYLD disc Jockey; Mike Early, WWL General Manager; Mel Leavitt, Mary Lou Mack, (for her late husband, sportscaster Wayne Mack), and Phil Johnson.

Following "Nut and Jeff" on WSMB Radio each morning was Keith Rush, who hosted a talk show. He interviewed coaches, politicians, writers, and other celebs around town.

Then in the wee hours of the morning, Radio Hall of Famer Larry Regan entertained the up-all-night crowd. Larry had colorful characters calling in, feuding and sounding off with each other as Larry refereed, taking a humorous approach to these eccentrics and insomniacs. There was the "Yankee Clipper," who had a wooden leg, diabetes, a whiskey voice, and went to the opera and the balls. There was Garnishee Joe and Mr. Black, who was white. There was "Understanding Henry," who booked horses out of a doughnut shop; "Shirley the Alcoholic," who dipped her toast in vodka so she wouldn't get drunk on an empty stomach; and the Parakeet, a street-wise little woman, a natural comedienne. Larry made them funny and encouraged them to call back, and listeners waited to hear them.

On WWL, a competitor to Nut and Jeff was Bob Ruby, whose gimmick was that he rang a pay phone out on the street and talked to whoever answered. Also at WWL was Sid Noel, who was then a disc jockey. Herb Holiday was the host of *Midday* on WWL. And in the afternoon, Charlie Briant was another disc jockey.

WDSU Radio started something new and innovative in the sixties. General Manager Hal Wheelahan raised money to rent a helicopter from which to do traffic reports during drive time. He called on Tony Bonagera of the police department to do these reports, and Tony is still doing them. This station, like all the others, played music, broadcast news, sports, and weather, and did its best to introduce live personalities who competed in entertaining their audiences with lively talk and interviews.

Bob and Jan Carr, standing right, interviewed guests in the Plantation Room at the Roosevelt (now the Fairmont) as part of their radio program *Second Cup*, for WWL. Standing left is Charlie Mills, manager of the Plantation Room. Seated, third, fourth, and fifth from left are executives of WWL Al Widmer, Bill Dean, and Walter Bouche. (Courtesy Al Widmer)

Roy Roberts (Roy Makofsky), seated, and Jeff Hug, standing, billed as "Nut and Jeff" on WSMB Radio early morning dress-and-drive time, were the first and most popular talk show hosts on radio in the sixties and long after. (Courtesy Gerry Makofsky)

BOOKS OF THE SIXTIES—BETTY FRIEDAN SAYS, "MAKE POLICY, NOT COFFEE."

Betty Naomi Goldstein Friedan's book, *The Feminine Mystique*, released in 1963, caused a revolution in thinking among women. Her book declared that women, as a class, suffered a variety of subtle and not-so-subtle forms of discrimination. She argued strongly that women were urged to find personal fulfillment vicariously through their husbands and children, to whom they were expected to cheerfully devote their lives. "This wife-mother role," she wrote, "led . . . to a sense of . . . unreality or general spiritual malaise in the absence of genuine, creative, self-defining work."

In October 1966, Friedan co-founded the National Organization for Women (NOW), a civil-rights group dedicated to achieving equality of opportunity for women. As president of NOW, she directed campaigns to end sex-classified employment practices, to have greater representation of women in government, to have child-care centers for working mothers, and to promote legalized abortion. She said that the National Women's Political Caucus was organized "to make policy, not coffee."

An example of the kind of resentment Friedan stirred up in women was the trashing of bras and high heels (instruments of oppression) that took place when a Miss America contest was held. She had convinced her followers that the parading of women for the judgment of their figures and feminine charms was the worst kind of degradation.

She wanted the women of America to stand up and tell the world they were dissatisfied with their lives. She wanted them to take up the standard and march in the women's revolution. The time for it was perfect. Negroes were demanding integration, not only in schools, but in all public places, and in government. Youth was rebelling against the war, against their parents, against the state the world was in, against the Establishment in general. So the time was rife for women to say they were equal to men and they intended to prove it in the workplace and in politics.

Most of the New Orleans women I knew were not avid followers of Betty Friedan. It was hard to light a revolutionary fire under Southern women when it came to changing the status quo. And being predominantly Catholic, most New Orleans women were against her pro-choice doctrine concerning abortion. Perhaps it was also the languid climate of this slow-to-change city that made it lag behind in a sexual revolution.

Betty didn't fit into my plans at all. I found no personal fulfillment in having to get up at 6:00 in the morning, shower, dress, make breakfast for four, fill brown bags for lunch, take out something to defrost for evening supper, and be out of the house and standing before a class of 30 semi-happy children by 8:00 in the morning. I taught school when the income was necessary. But when finances permitted, I was happy to be a stay-at-home mom who could do things in her own time, cook at leisure, fold clothes while I watched my soaps, take a nap, join in coffee klatches with my neighbors, and do a little gardening and free-lance writing. I had no desire to surpass any man in the work place. But that was just me.

LOCAL AUTHORS

The careers of Walker Percy and Shirley Ann Grau took off in the sixties with the publications of Percy's *The Moviegoer* and Grau's *The Keepers of the House*.

In *The Keepers of the House*, which won a Pulitzer prize in 1965, Grau wrote about seven generations of the Howland family who inhabited, defended, and expanded the land and the house overlooking it. She wrote about the South with love and pride. Some of her other books were *The Black Prince, The Hard Blue Sky, The House on Coliseum Street,* and *The Condor Passes.*

Walker Percy, a native of Mississippi, lived in New Orleans for a while. He found the city overwhelming, however, and settled in Covington, where he found peace and quiet to write many eminently successful books. His novel, *The Moviegoer,* set in New Orleans, won the 1962 National Book Award for Fiction. Among his other books were *The Last Gentleman* and *Love in the Ruins.*

Lillian Hellman, often called America's premiere woman playwright, grew up in New Orleans. She enjoyed success in the theater for 30 years, beginning with her daring play *The Children's Hour* in 1934 and continuing through 1960 with her autobiographical play, *Toys in the Attic.* Her other works included *The Little Foxes* and *Another Part of the Forest.*

Katherine Anne Porter, a Texas native, lived in New Orleans as a teenager, moved away for some years, and moved back to New Orleans in 1937. She lived in the Pontalba Apartments in the French Quarter. After writing such memorable books as *Flowering Judas; Pale Horse, Pale Rider;* and *The Days Before,* she wrote the best selling *Ship of Fools* in 1962. It was made into a highly successful movie.

John Kennedy Toole wrote his Pulitzer Prize-winning novel *Confederacy of Dunces* in the early sixties. The story of the author is a tragic one, which reads like a novel itself. Toole was a man of many talents. He was a brilliant mathematician, a cartoonist for the *Hullabaloo* at Tulane, a man with an extraordinary ear for dialects, and a lover of movies and the theater. He taught at Tulane University, always waiting to have enough time to devote to writing. In 1961, he was drafted into the military and spent two years in Puerto Rico, where he finally wrote his novel. In 1964, he began submitting it to New York publishers. After several rejections, he sent it to Simon and Schuster, where a senior editor first accepted, then later rejected it. Before the final rejection, however, Toole had been asked to do a number of rewrites, which he willingly did.

Totally despondent after his final rejection, he took his own life. His mother shopped the manuscript around for years and finally presented it to Walker Percy, who found himself amazed and enchanted with the work. He had it retyped and sent it to LSU Press in Baton Rouge, where it was released in 1980. *Confederacy of Dunces* won a Pulitzer Prize in 1981.

Toole's ear for New Orleans dialects, and his gift for capturing the essence of local characters, were at last recognized with the highest possible tribute, but it was too late for the talented writer. A statue of his principal character, Ignatius O'Reilly, with mustache and baseball cap, stands on Canal Street, where the famous clock at D. H. Holmes department store used to be. In *Confederacy of Dunces,* Ignatius stood beneath the clock waiting, as New Orleanians had for decades, to meet a friend. The clock is now in the Clock Bar inside the Chateau Sonesta, which replaced D. H. Holmes.

CHAPTER TWELVE

Politics—
The Accidental Mayor

LET ME START OFF by saying that I loved Mayor Victor Schiro. If I call him "The Accidental Mayor," I do so with affection. Alec Gifford of WDSU-TV used the term in reference to Mayor Schiro in a recent documentary. He asked if we remembered the movie, *The Accidental Tourist.* "Well, that's what Schiro was," he said, "the accidental mayor." Schiro was Councilman-at-large on the City Council when Mayor Morrison resigned in 1961 to accept his appointment as Ambassador to the Organization of the American States. To fill the vacancy, the City Council voted Schiro the interim mayor. But he was elected twice, in 1962 and 1966, so he had undoubtedly proven himself a progressive and popular mayor.

MORRISON AND LANDRIEU: BOOKENDS FOR SCHIRO

Schiro dominated politics in New Orleans in the sixties. But Mayor deLesseps S. ("Chep") Morrison served as mayor till 1961 and Maurice ("Moon") Landrieu was prominent enough in politics to be elected mayor in 1969. It is hard to talk about Schiro without referring to one of the other two. Morrison and Landrieu influenced Schiro's political life before, during, and after its many crises. To view the entire decade, we must review the politics of all three men.

MAYOR MORRISON, CAUGHT IN A CRISIS

Mayor Morrison, a young, handsome, popular veteran of World War II, had served as mayor for 16 years when he resigned in 1961. Although he was very successful in politics in New Orleans, he was defeated in his bid for governor three times, rejected by northern Louisianians who staunchly opposed New Orleanians in politics, partly due to their Catholicsm. As mayor, he set the city on a new track of integrity in government. During his four terms, he made the Port of New Orleans a competitor with Miami as the "Gateway to Latin America." He expanded tourism and brought in new industry.

Mayor Victor Schiro, center, with city councilmen (1961-1969). Standing, left to right: Henry Curtis, Walter Marcus, Clarence Dupuy, John Petre, and Daniel Kelly; seated, left to right: Joseph DiRosa, Mayor Schiro, and James Fitzmorris. (Courtesy New Orleans Public Library)

So many underpasses and overpasses were built during his administrations, to eliminate hazardous railway and vehicular crossings, that he was called "The Overpass King."

He replaced a city slum area with a city, state, and federal building complex, including the present City Hall. He pushed through the 24-mile-long Lake Pontchartrain Causeway in 1956 and the Greater New Orleans Mississippi River Bridge in 1958. Yet this advanced and intelligent leader remained silent on the most critical social problem his city faced: the racial desegregation of its schools in 1960.

MORRISON PROTECTS HIS IMAGE

Throughout the integration controversy, Morrison clung to the 60-year-old Plessey v. Ferguson "separate but equal" doctrine in schools, which he apparently considered liberal enough to guarantee his popularity. But in the late fifties, demands were made of Judge J. Skelly Wright to put some teeth into his ruling of 1956 that segregation in public schools was illegal (see chapter two). Now Morrison's feet were to the fire.

At that juncture, he was planning to run for governor for the second time and he knew he needed the segregationists for his political future. "I have nothing to do with the operation of the schools," he reminded his constituents at every opportunity. "My duty is to protect life and property and maintain law and order." The citizens of New Orleans knew this was true, yet some hoped he would nevertheless do more. He blamed the explosive situation on agitators like Leander Perez, Senator Rainach, and the news media.

After his appearance on national television, on the program *Face the Nation*, on November 21, 1960, the majority of letters the mayor received supported his actions during the crisis. But Morrison's failure to act had created a leadership void that had allowed racial extremists on both sides to seize control, and he had alienated large segments of the voting public.

On May 22, 1964, Morrison was in a chartered plane flying to Mexico on a combined business and pleasure trip with his young son, Randy. His plane crashed into a mountain, killing them both and bringing his career to an untimely end.

BACKGROUND ON MAYOR VICTOR H. SCHIRO

Mayor Schiro was born of an Italian father who had been involved in banking business in Honduras. Young Victor spent much of his childhood in Honduras, where he learned to speak Spanish, a language that was of great value to him when he was mayor, traveling to Central America. As a young man, he attended Tulane University and graduated from Santa Clara in California.

A HOLLYWOOD ACTOR? I DIDN'T KNOW THAT!

I wonder how many of you readers knew that Schiro worked as an actor under the highly acclaimed director William Wyler for three years after finishing college. I didn't know it. He scored some points with me when I heard it. His career, like those of many actors, was cut short by World War II, in which he served three years in the Coast Guard. After the war, he came home and tried many different lines of work: radio announcer, program director, and insurance salesman. Then he opened an insurance company of his own. He is also well known for his work on more than one Frank Capra movie as a cameraman.

Mayor Schiro and wife Sunny about to leave on a trip to Mexico with (on left)
Joseph M. Rault, Jr. and Mrs. Rault and (on right) Congressman T. Hale Boggs
and Lindy Boggs. (Courtesy New Orleans Public Library)

SCHIRO'S FIRST SORTIE INTO POLITICS

Victor Schiro's first effort in politics was his vigorous support of a Home Rule Charter, adopted in 1954. The charter set up a clear-cut separation of legislative and administrative powers in New Orleans by replacing the old Commission Council form of government with the new mayor-council type. The mayor, no longer a member of the council, was thereafter solely responsible for the administration of the government. Thereby, executive authority was vested in one elected official. The mayor had a chief administrative officer, who supervised all thirteen departments, and a council of seven men, who constituted a purely legislative body. Two years later, in 1956, Home Rule was declared one of the most efficient city governments in the country.

Mayor Morrison endorsed Schiro in his candidacy for City Council, and he was elected in 1950. In two successive elections, 1954 and 1958, he was elected Councilman-at-large. Then finally, he took over the office of mayor when Morrison resigned in 1961.

SCHIRO INHERITS SCHOOL INTEGRATION PROBLEM

In the fall of 1961, the same school integration crisis existed that had plagued Mayor Morrison in 1960. It was not about to go away. The episodes of rock throwing and cursing the black children entering white schools in 1960 had brought national criticism against New Orleans. As we have said, Mayor Schiro ordered the police to set up barricades to keep segregationists a good distance from the children. Thus demonstrations were avoided, photographers had nothing to photograph, and integration proceeded more smoothly.

Schiro ended segregation of restrooms at City Hall. He appointed the first black executive assistant to the mayor's office, and was the first mayor to sanction the appointment of blacks as heads of important boards and commissions since the end of Reconstruction. These changes in racial tolerance and good will were exactly what the city needed to prevent the racial upheavals that were occurring elsewhere in the South in cities with large black populations.

THE SPACE PROGRAM DURING SCHIRO'S ADMINISTRATION

During Schiro's administration, New Orleans' importance in the space race skyrocketed with the successful launching of the first three Saturn boosters assembled at NASA's Michoud Assembly Facility. The facility brought thousands of technicians, engineers, and administrators to Michoud, which was just fifteen minutes away from downtown New Orleans. In 1965, contracts with firms operating at Michoud were valued at more than $1.5 billion. Of that amount, $57 million were in construction contracts, of which $40 million were awarded to companies in the New Orleans area.

In 1965, Michoud employed some 10,400, with a combined payroll of about $94 million. This meant new households, increased retail sales, and an expanded tax base. Ours was a thriving economy, and Mayor Schiro smiled and enjoyed it.

SCHIRO ON HURRICANE BETSY AND THE DOMED STADIUM

During Hurricane Betsy in 1965, the most devastating hurricane to reach the United States until that time, it was Schiro's prompt and effective coordination of relief efforts that played the most important role in the city's recovery.

107

Schiro was mayor when plans for the construction of the Domed Stadium (Superdome) were on the table. He supported all initial plans, as well as the bond amendment in the November 8, 1966, election for raising the millions needed for the construction of the stadium.

SCHIRO MAKES NEW ORLEANS AN INTERNATIONAL CITY

Despite setbacks at home like Hurricane Betsy, Schiro kept his eye on the international picture, which loomed larger than ever in 1965. In December, he visited the heads of state of Nicaragua, El Salvador, Guatemala, Honduras, and Costa Rica for talks leading to an establishment of New Orleans as a proposed common market between Central America and the United States. Earlier in the year, the mayor had received the Order of Isabella la Catolica, Spain's highest decoration. He was presented the rank of Commendador in the Order at the residence of Spain's ambassador to the United States.

THE CITY CHANGES FACE

While Schiro was in office, the city changed face, adding its own beautification to that of Morrison's era, including the rebuilding of Poydras Street and the construction of the Rivergate and the ITM Building. The riverfront docks began to come down as part of the 30-year plan of the port to move them in the direction of New Orleans East.

MAYOR MAURICE ("MOON") LANDRIEU, A MAN OF PRINCIPLE

Since Mayor "Moon" Landrieu's administration did not begin until 1970, which brings us into another decade, we will mention here only his political activities of the sixties. Landrieu, a lawyer, a veteran, the father of nine children, became active in the Young Crescent City Democratic Association in the late fifties. This was an organization aligned with the CCDA led by Mayor Morrison. With Morrison's endorsement, he had won a seat in the State House of Representatives.

In 1960, when Governor Jimmie Davis convened a special session of the state legislature to consider a package of pro-segregationist bills to get around the federal court orders to integrate New Orleans Public Schools, Landrieu was the only member of the Louisiana House of Representatives to put principle before expediency and vote against the bills. This courageous move brought on death threats, but in the middle and late sixties, his support of equal rights proved to be an asset. In 1965, he won a seat on the City Council as Councilman-at-Large. And, in 1969, he was elected mayor.

LOUISIANA GOVERNORS OF THE SIXTIES

On April 19, 1960, Jimmie "You Are my Sunshine" Davis was elected governor of Louisiana. It was his lap into which Mayor Morrison dropped the "hot potato" of school integration in New Orleans. Davis, a staunch supporter of segregation, willingly asked the legislature to enact laws that would prohibit the allocation of funds to integrated schools and allow the governor to close the schools "to prevent violence" (see chapter two). The legislators passed 29 separate acts, and Judge J. Skelly Wright kept his court open day and night to throw them out as they passed before him.

VIPs in hard hats at the construction site of the Superdome are, left to right: A. L. Davis, Governor John J. McKeithen, Tom Donelon, president of Jefferson Parish, Dave Dixon, Mayor-elect Moon Landrieu, outgoing Mayor Vic Schiro, and Senator Hank Lauricello. (Courtesy Moon and Verna Landrieu)

On August 17, 1960, as we have seen, Governor Davis assumed control of Orleans Parish public schools. But on August 27, a three-judge panel issued a temporary restraining order against the governor and restored control of the schools to the Orleans Parish School Board.

In 1962, when President Kennedy came to New Orleans to dedicate the Nashville Street wharf, he was hosted by Governor Davis and Mayor Schiro, not a meaningful accomplishment for the governor, but there wasn't much more you could say about Jimmie Davis. As governor, he spent most of his time flying back and forth to Hollywood, acting with his country-western band in "B" movies. His own political rallies consisted of playing and singing his country songs for his constituents, and making sure there were lots of crawfish on hand. Jimmie was one of the "good ole boys."

John J. McKeithen, elected in 1964, re-elected in 1967, was to serve out the rest of the decade as governor. His views on integration were decidedly negative at the outset of his administration, but he was forced to change with the times to save his political career. By 1965, for the first time in 90 years, there were two Republicans on the floor of the Louisiana House of Representatives. Eisenhower had carried the state in 1956 and Goldwater in 1964. Republican candidate Charlton Lyons had polled 40 percent of the statewide vote against McKeithen. John McKeithen recognized these changes from liberal to conservative political attitudes, and he began to bend. From a staunch segregationist, he became a moderate. He subverted violence at Bogalusa in 1965. He pushed for a code of ethics and asked for reconciliation and unity.

Governor McKeithen gave his endorsement to the Domed Stadium, gambling his political future. But in 1967, the voters approved both the stadium and a second term for McKeithen.

CHAPTER THIRTEEN

Doubloons and Super Krewes

To New Orleanians, Mardi Gras is a day of fun, but Carnival is also a season of endless celebrations. Although we are happy to share it with the world, we consider it our very own New Orleans party.

A DELIGHT TO CHILDREN, TEENS, AND PARENTS

As children, my siblings and I were always dressed in costume and taken to my grandfather's office on the third floor of the Audubon Building on Canal Street to view the Rex Parade, then brought to City Park to have our pictures taken on one of the lions on the steps of the peristyle or on the cannon outside the Delgado Museum.

As pre-teens and teenagers, we attended king cake parties, where the guest who picked the piece of cake with the doll inside got to be the host of the party the following week (good news for the winner's mother). The King Cake tradition had its roots in Medieval Europe as a religious celebration. The cycle of time for the parties began on Kings' Day, January 6, which is the twelfth night after the birth of Jesus, when the Three Kings presented gifts to the Christ Child, and continued until Ash Wednesday, the beginning of Lent. The cake for this celebration contained a hidden object (a gift), and the reveler who got the "gift" became the King and gave the next party. The first documented connection between Mardi Gras and the King Cake came on January 6, 1870, at the first ball of the Carnival organization known as the Twelfth Night Revelers. Over the years, the item tucked inside the cake has included coins, peas, pecans, and dolls.

As teenagers and young adults after World War II, we rode with friends on flatbed trucks, costumed in the theme of the truck, which followed the Rex Parade on Mardi Gras Day. Two truck parades, Elks and Orleanians, grew longer and more elaborate each year. I recall a truck we rode on in the late forties called "Patricks and Cute Tricks," in which we dressed as lads and lassies of the Emerald Isle. Many trucks had Dixieland bands, but ours was not so fancy. An artist

Doubloons were as collectible as jewels in the sixties.

designed a rainbow for the top of our truck, with an Irish leprechaun doing a jig among a few four-leaf clovers. We brought our lunch and an ice chest of drinks and that was it—no sanitary facilities. We relied on stops at grocery stores or ice-houses for the use of bathrooms. This was when truck parades were just beginning. By the sixties, many trucks were marvels of ingenuity that challenged the beauty of the parade itself, and were fitted out with every conceivable convenience.

As long as the old-line krewes—Momus, Comus, Proteus, Rex, and Hermes—paraded through the narrow streets of the French Quarter and Faubourg St. Mary, the floats were necessarily small. And because there was no other way to illuminate the parades in the early decades of the century, flambeau carriers in white sheets strutted alongside the floats, twirling their torch-bearing poles. But as time went by, innovations came thick and fast each year.

CHANGES OVER THE DECADES

As far back as the thirties, Hermes introduced neon lighting to illuminate its floats. But most krewes preferred to continue using the traditional and colorful flambeaux carriers. In the forties, Mid-City, a daytime parade, added gleaming aluminum foil to its papier-mâché floats. In those days, the parade route of the old organizations began at Felicity Street and rolled up St. Charles Avenue, turned left at Canal Street, and then right at Rampart to the Municipal Auditorium, where all the Carnival krewes staged their balls for decades.

In the fifties, tractors replaced the city sanitation department mules in the Thoth parade. In the fifties and sixties, we began to see ladders with seats on top for small children to view the parades from sidewalks and neutral grounds, without breaking their fathers' shoulders.

Pete Fountain, Grand Marshal of his own parade, strutted his way down Canal Street in the early sixties. To the right is his father, Peter Dewey Fountain, Sr. Behind him, the Onward brass Band. (Courtesy Pete Fountain)

Before Herbert Grant Jahncke climbed up to begin his reign as Rex on February 22, 1966, he called his mother who was unable to attend because of a hip injury. "This is the king speaking, Mom," he said, to which she replied, "Have a good ride, Son." And then she added, "And, Son, don't fall off that float."

Opposite: Herbert Grant Jahncke, Rex of 1966, greets his Queen at the Boston Club. His great-grandfather Fritz Jahncke, the "sand and gravel man," came to New Orleans in 1872, the year of the first Rex parade. Fritz's son served as Rex in 1915; his granddaughter Cora as Queen of Rex in 1936; and his great-grandson Herbert as Rex in 1966.

OUR CHOSEN SPOT FOR MARDI GRAS IN THE SIXTIES

For years in the fifties and sixties, my husband and I and a couple of close friends, with their children and ours, viewed the Rex parade from a spot on the neutral ground on St. Charles Avenue and Conery Street. We chose this spot because we were allowed bathroom privileges by a friend who lived nearby. The night before Mardi Gras, we parked one of our cars, with folding chairs inside, as well as iced drinks and a picnic lunch, on a street close to our chosen location.

Then, on Mardi Gras morning, in a second car, we found a parking place as close to our destination as possible and walked to the car we'd parked the night before. We took out our chairs, our food and drinks, and ensconced ourselves for the day on the neutral ground on St. Charles Avenue, where we could view the Rex parade, as it passed no more than 15 feet away. It was ideal. No streetcars would run that day, so our children could run about on the neutral ground without danger.

But nothing good lasts forever. And, we discovered there was nothing so brilliant about our plans. Each year, we found ourselves more and more thickly surrounded by a forest of ladders, as well as playpens, sofas, and folding tables. In the center of so many tall obstructions, our children could no longer see the floats or catch throws from the riders. In addition, our friend's house had become so overrun by dangerous looking characters, she'd been forced to hire a security guard to stop people from coming in. We finally gave up our lovely spot.

The population grew, and parades became more spectacular. Viewers took over every neutral ground in the city and fitted out spots for their comfort while watching a parade that would pass along that route. On Orleans Avenue, for example, the night before the Endymion parade, families and friends began staking out their "spots," carrying out recliners, lamps (with very long cords), card tables, chairs, mattresses, food, and drinks. Individuals take turns holding these treasured stake-outs, where they will have a good view of the parade, be able to catch many throws, and be as comfortable as if they were in their own living rooms. Fortunately, in New Orleans, the weather usually cooperates. It is a worthwhile experience to drive alongside these neutral grounds, if you can find passage, on the morning of the parade and witness "Mardi Gras on the neutral grounds," our own version of Woodstock. And no matter what you do, don't forget your camera!

MARDI GRAS SPREADS OUT TO THE SUBURBS

By the sixties, the heart of the city was no longer a pleasant place for old time Carnival lovers to view Rex or any other parade. Organizations that paraded in the suburbs and the nearby towns of Covington, Algiers, Gretna, and Slidell offered less crowded parade viewing, at least when they were new.

CHANGES IN THE SIXTIES

In 1960, a new "throw" appeared, one that was to become a tradition in the annals of Mardi Gras. It was called a doubloon, and it was struck with the image of Rex himself and thrown by the riders of the Rex parade. The designer was an artist named H. Alvin Sharpe. Each year thereafter, more and more carnival organizations had their own doubloons, in a variety of colors, impressed with the emblems of their organizations. Doubloon collectors kept boxes and binders and specially designed plastic sheets with pockets for doubloons of all krewes in all colors, and paid big money to keep their collections complete.

Pete Fountain's Half-Fast Walking Club started in 1961. This was a year when members dressed as Dutch boys. Center, with trumpet, is Frank Minyard, coroner. Second from right (with beads), is Paul Sita, author's brother-in-law. (Courtesy Paul Sita)

117

Members of another organization, the Krewe of Grela, threw a coin-like object that same year, 1960, and did so three days before Rex threw its first doubloons. These were the famous Grela krewe-emblemed wooden nickels.

BACCHUS, THE FIRST SUPER KREWE

In 1968, twelve New Orleans businessmen met to discuss innovative changes for Carnival clubs to breathe new life into Mardi Gras and bring more tourists into the city. In 1969, the Krewe of Bacchus paraded for the first time on the Sunday night before Mardi Gras, breaking many traditions, and leaving New Orleanians and tourists wide-eyed with wonder.

Larry Youngblood, costume designer for the Krewe of Bacchus since its inception, displays some of his creations. (Courtesy Owen Brennan, captain of Bacchus)

Danny Kaye, the first Bacchus, greets his subjects at the Rivergate in 1969.
(Courtesy Owen Brennan, captain of Bacchus)

LOCATION: THE RIVERGATE

The Bacchus organization presented to the public the largest floats ever assembled, followed by a dance in the Rivergate, taking the place of the tableaux and the King's Supper dances of the old organizations. The mammoth floats formed a circle inside the Rivergate, serving as a backdrop for the tables-for-ten, occupied by escorts and friends of Bacchus riders. Inside the hall, the Bacchus organization offered Las Vegas-style entertainment followed by general dancing and a breakfast. And instead of naming a member of an old-line society family as king, they offered the crown to a Hollywood celebrity.

Revelers surrounded by enormous Bacchus floats prepare to enjoy entertainment and an early morning breakfast at the Rivergate, 1969. (Courtesy Owen Brennan, captain of Bacchus)

THE FIRST BACCHUS PARTY

My husband and I were invited to the very first Bacchus ball, as guests of a business friend who rode in the parade. The party didn't begin until almost midnight, but it was worth the wait. We had to be inside the Rivergate before the parade arrived, so we did not get to see the floats parading in the streets to the clamor of thousands. We caught our first glimpse of them when they pulled into the building and surrounded us, one gargantuan float after another. We screamed and applauded and shouted with absolute delight as King Kong, more monstrous than the original, entered the enormous building with arms extended and jaw agape, his teeth bared in a frightening growl. Another signature float that became a trademark was Bacchusaurus, the dinosaur.

The god Bacchus who ruled over the first parade and ball was Danny Kaye. I remember his speech. "I have been to many places and seen many things in my life, but I have never seen anything to compare to this." The people in the Rivergate went wild. Among the Bacchus gods of later years were Bob Hope, Jackie Gleason, and Charlton Heston.

Ladies danced with members of the krewe to the music of not one but three alternating Jazz and Dixieland Bands and everyone went "second-linin'" around the floor, waving handkerchiefs and following a New Orleans brass band.

Later on, a beautiful breakfast of grits and eggs and sausages was served, with café-au-lait, New Orleans style.

VIEW OF HERMES PARADE FROM
KOLB'S SECOND STORY BALCONY

In the sixties, WSMB Radio invited all its station employees and their spouses to a formal dinner at Kolb's, a famous old German restaurant (now closed) on St. Charles Avenue and Canal Street on the night of the Hermes parade. This is how my husband and I got to enjoy a sumptuous meal, followed by a view of the parade from Kolb's second-story balcony. On that chilly Friday night before Mardi Gras, as we waited for the parade in our evening gowns and warm wraps, the waiter circulated, refilling our glasses with champagne. Talk about elegance!

Finally, in the distance, we saw the brightly illuminated head of the snake curling its way around Lee Circle, then turning tortuously into St. Charles Avenue, its music getting louder and louder until the parade was directly below us. The bands played and the *flambeaux* carriers strutted in the cold night. People in the street down below shouted for beads and trinkets, but no more than we did. The krewe members seemed to enjoy tossing handfuls of beads up to the balconies. It was a Mardi Gras experience never to be forgotten.

Like most New Orleanians, we had viewed parades from sidewalks and neutral grounds, porches and balconies, with and without children, in large groups and on our own. This happens when you live in New Orleans and you love Mardi Gras . . . but this was a rare treat.

ENDYMION, A MAIN EVENT OF MARDI GRAS

Many who read this will wonder why Endymion was not mentioned before Bacchus, since it was organized in 1967. The reason is that Endymion began as a small neighborhood organization, with floats borrowed from the Carrollton parade. Fulfilling the dream of its young captain, Ed Muniz, the driving force behind Endymion, who wanted to fill the Saturday night before Mardi Gras on

Endymion I, Harry P. Rosenthal, prepares to toast his queen in the krewe's inaugural parade in 1967. (Courtesy Ed Muniz, captain of Endymion)

the Carnival calendar, Endymion first rolled on February 4, 1967. For ten years, it started at the intersection of Trafalgar and DeSaix Boulevards, near Bayou St. John and the Fairgrounds racetrack. By 1974, however, it had grown into an extravaganza to rival Bacchus with gargantuan floats and celebrity monarchs. It, too, provided lavish entertainment to its viewers.

Endymion I, Harry P. Rosenthal, poses with his royal dukes, left to right: San Nicholas, Charles Wall, Leon Walle, Benny Zimmerman, John Toussel, Sam Cimino, Jr., Donald Wilson, and Lloyd Bowers. (Courtesy Ed Muniz, captain of Endymion)

CHAPTER FOURTEEN

Fashions, Hairdos, and Fads

WE, THE SILENT MAJORITY non-hippies, the ladies who followed fashion as far as our credit cards allowed, had First Lady Jackie Kennedy as our trendsetter at the outset of the decade. Her styles were simple, yet elegant, and manufacturers could copy the designer models for half the price, so that every woman in America could be a Jackie look-alike. In her pillbox hat, her sleeveless sheath, and her low-heeled pumps, she created a fashion style that women wore throughout the sixties and beyond.

Another typical "Jackie" outfit was the suit with the slender knee-length skirt and the short jacket with three-quarter-length sleeves worn with gauntlet gloves. Her styles were exquisite in their simplicity, even to the formal white satin gown and cape she wore to the inaugural ball. For formal occasions, she went bare headed, her shining black hair done up in a bouffant pageboy, crowning her out-fit more beautifully than any hat or veil.

The Duchess of Windsor followed Jackie's style, as did television actress Marlo Thomas in *That Girl*, and Doris Day in light romantic comedies like *Pillow Talk*.

AUDREY HEPBURN WAS AN ORIGINAL

Audrey Hepburn, born the same year as Jackie, wore almost the identical styles, not in imitation of Jackie, for Audrey herself was an original. Both Jackie and Audrey were tall and slender, had excellent posture, wore clothes like mannequins, and knew what looked good on them. As a result, their "look" was very similar.

Audrey was such an original that her style came to be called "Audrey Style." A peek in her closet might reveal the little black dress, the sleeveless sheath dress, Capri pants, a dark turtleneck, jeans and sneakers, basic flat shoes, a Givenchy dressy dress to knock your eyes out, a pair of low-heel sling-back Sabrina shoes, Hermes scarves to wear over the head and around the neck, and huge dark sun-glasses. Her jewelry was minimal. To Audrey, elegance was in simplicity, or, as we say today, less was more. The fashion world revered her as an icon.

Bridal group of the sixties—bride is author's sister, Terry Schultis Sita. Clockwise: Danny Muro, Anne LaRocca, Gerry Burger, Cheryl Smith, Sandra Difatta, and flower girl Dana Widmer, author's daughter. (Courtesy Terry Sita)

MARY TYLER MOORE, A SIXTIES "STAY-AT-HOME" MOM

One more fashion leader I'd like to call to memory is actress-dancer-singer Mary Tyler Moore, who dressed very much like Jackie and Audrey. When she was asked if she'd play the stay-at-home mom on *The Dick Van Dyke Show*, she said she would die for the part, but she wouldn't wear house dresses and pearls and high heels at breakfast. She'd wear what she always wore at home—Capri pants, turtleneck pullovers, and flat ballet shoes. This was how we saw her in the very first episode of *The Dick Van Dyke Show* and we loved her. Her "look" validated the "look" of every housewife in America as she cooked dinner or made beds.

FURS WERE WORN WITH MIXED FEELINGS

This was the decade when we were all becoming environmentally aware. It had crept up on us in the fifties, but now we were reading every day about certain

Models for a fashion show line up outside a New Orleans building, awaiting transportation to the hotel where they will model styles of the sixties.

animals becoming endangered species, and we began thinking about the future in which our children and grandchildren would live. Would there be any forests left? Would there be any animals in them? Would the atmosphere be one they could breathe without an oxygen tank? Would there be fish in the sea, after all the pollution and oil spills? We were told to stop killing animals just to keep ourselves warm. Some of us had furs and had planned to wear them for the next twenty years. We pinched our lips and gave it some thought. After all, the animals were dead already, and the money had been spent. Hmmm.

Older ladies paid little attention and went right on wearing their furs. Young and middle-aged women were of two minds about it. But those in the public eye who were supposed to give example—Jackie Kennedy, Queen Elizabeth, the Duchess of Windsor—wore their "good cloth coats" dressed up with crown collars and adorned with triple chokers of pearls. They concentrated on jewelry and elaborate bouffant hairdos and gloves and handbags to dress up the basic coats.

WHAT WERE CROWN COLLARS, YOU ASK?

Crown collars, extremely popular in the sixties, were put on cloth coats to circle the lady's face, not at the neck like a choker, but two inches away from the face, like a circular frame. I had a soldier blue wool coat, with a swing hemline and a cerulean blue mink crown collar that I wore for ten years. It was beautiful. Soft as silk and luxurious. Even suits and dresses had crown collars. They were flattering to the face and we loved them.

JUST FOR FUN, PRICES ON A CHRISTMAS SALE

Misses' pure woolen coats and suits, regularly $24.95, sale price $15.00.
Pure wool dresses—sheaths, shifts, dressy, casual, reg. $8.95, sale price $5.00.
Casual twill car coat, collared in acrylic pile, quilted lining, reg. $12.95, sale price $7.88.
Men's dress shirts, reg. $2.99, on sale 2 for $5.00

HAIRDOS AND HATS

If you were a teenager, or in your early twenties, you wore your hair long and straight, or possibly turned up at the shoulder-length ends in a big sweeping curl (a la Marlo Thomas in *That Girl*). The teenager might have her mom iron her hair on the ironing board, very carefully. For the turn up curl at the shoulder, she rolled up her hair on orange juice cans. With long hair, she wore the obligatory headband. Long, straight hair was often worn with bangs, either thick down to the eyebrows or swept to the side, with the headband and the teased crown of hair behind the headband.

If you were over twenty-five, you wore your hair short. Here again you could choose from a variety of hairdos. Hairstyles were no longer as severe as in the fifties, when the hairline was shingled, and only a forward curl over the ear relieved the mannish look. In the sixties, hairdos became softer, fuller, much bigger, and more feminine.

A popular style was a full short hairdo, in which the hair was cut about two inches below the ear, rolled under in a short page boy with a forward curl on the face. This could be tucked behind the ear or worn over the ear. It was worn with heavy bangs swept to one side of the forehead.

Diane Siebenkittel

Joan Relle

Patty Milazzo

Kathy Polit

Teenage hairstyles of the sixties.

129

TO DO THE HAIRDO

In the early sixties, women did their own hair in curlers, the center curls rolled back, the side curls down toward the ears. Anyone could do it if she had strong arms and a half-hour to kill. Then she would sit beneath her console "clamp-onto-the-table" hair dryer, and read for another half-hour or take a nap. Then came brushing the hair, teasing it unmercifully, arranging it in the preferred hairstyle, and spraying it with lacquer (another 45 minutes). The end result was a no-part hairstyle that was brushed back from the forehead and styled full over the ear, ending in a bouffant pageboy or a turn up at the ends. And it was monsoon-proof.

It was no wonder women began flocking to hair stylists and paying their weekly $8.00 to "have their hair done."

PRIDE GOETH WITH A FALL

Falls were lengths of hair in your own color that could be pinned to the crown of the head and combed over and through your own hair to give it more thickness

Teenage hairstyles and fashions of the sixties.

*Teenagers Evelyn Fabre and Connie Mayeaux, students of Holy Angels
Academy, take a catnap on the way home from drama competition in Lafayette
in 1967. Check out the hairdos, rollers, and bandanas.*

and length. For a very special evening, the fall could be styled first in a braided circle or a nest of soft curls and then pinned to the crown of the head. Another style with the fall was to pin it to the crown of the head and wrap it around the head like a bright, shining band (see Tippi Hedren in *The Birds*).

GOOD-BYE TO HATS

As the decade wore on, hairstyles became higher and more bouffant. More teasing and styling were necessary. As hairdos became bigger, hats were worn less often, since they smashed and flattened the hair. It was the beginning of the end for hats, which would disappear entirely in the seventies.

BATHING SUITS

Women wore one piece bathing suits in comfortable stretch fabrics like spandex. Two piece suits were also in style, but rarely were the pants cut below the navel. Bathing caps were out. In fact, at least half the female population stopped swimming altogether "to save the hairdo." Hairdos were time consuming and that took all the fun out of swimming. Except, of course, for teenagers who wore their hair straight. But all women continued to sit out in the sun and get a tan. No one worried about skin cancer. Bronze skin and a white dress! Wow! You couldn't beat it for glamour. Sun tan lotion was in, but sunscreen had not yet made the scene.

JEWELRY

Women wore chokers of pearls or gold, in single, double, and triple strands. They wore bangle bracelets, as many as five or six. (These were not for Jackie or Audrey or their followers). Earrings might be single pearls, or drop earrings in beads or gold. Pins were popular in the sixties, worn on the collar of the ubiquitous suit.

COSMETICS

Mascara and eye shadow became the most important cosmetics in the sixties. Heavy eye liner, double applications of mascara, and eyelids completely covered with blue or green or a mixture of colors painted beyond the side of the eyes gave a Cleopatra look that appealed especially to the teenagers and young twenties.

Foundation cream or liquid and cream rouge came into vogue. Back in the forties, make-up consisted of powder, rouge, and lipstick. A swipe with a moistened finger removed powder from your eyebrows and eyelashes. Only ladies with very blond lashes used mascara, usually Maybelline, which could be purchased at Woolworth's for just $0.10. It came in a tiny red box with its own little brush. But by the sixties, ladies were being told on television and in magazines that they could be a lot more beautiful. Max Factor of Hollywood was largely responsible for that.

MEN'S WEAR

Men still wore white dress shirts for work with a suit or sport coat and contrasting trousers. They wore white or colored dress shirts for night affairs. Ties were narrow; belts were narrow. It was a conservative decade for the well-dressed man. For a casual occasion, like a barbecue or a backyard party, they

This fashionable housewife wore a hairdo popular in the sixties with the extra-full bangs. Here she's showing off her side-by-side refrigerator with icemaker and huge storage doors.

wore button-down collared shirts, the top button open, the collar itself inside the collar of a coat or sweater. They wore plaid woolen shirts for football games or outdoor winter affairs. The cut of men's trousers was medium, neither full (like in the forties) nor tight-legged (only teenagers and The Beatles wore those).

For formal attire, they wore cuff links and studs and a black bow tie. Men's ascots appeared briefly in the early sixties. They were to be worn with a sport shirt, a coat, or a sweater. Somehow they never caught on. New Orleans was not an ascot town.

TEENAGE SKIRTS: SHORT, SHORTER, SHORTEST

My daughter-in-law was a teenager in the sixties. She says the skirts were so short they had to find a whole new way to sit down. Mini skirts were made with Indian fringes, some stamped with the sign of peace. Mignon Faget, later an acclaimed jewelry designer, turned out mini skirts with designs and fringe in the sixties. Mini skirts were worn with blouses or sweaters. Dresses themselves ended mid-thigh or higher. Wide hip-slung belts emphasized how little skirt was left below the belt.

With these skirts, go-go boots led the teen fashion world. Add to that—are you drawing this picture in your head?—long, straight hair, a headband, and heavy eye make-up. In this get-up, they danced on the John Pela *Saturday Afternoon Hop* and played guitar at Sunday Mass. Neither parents, priests, nor John Pela could make them change. Parents heard, "Well, everybody else dresses that way." John Pela couldn't fight thirty teenage girls. And priests were afraid they'd stop coming to mass. There was a lot of that going on in the sixties.

SCHOOL CLOTHES

For school, if it was Catholic school, girls wore white blouses and navy or gray skirts. The skirts were short, but a dress code dictated the number of inches of bare skin girls were allowed to show above the knee. The nuns also made the girls wear knee socks, which helped a little. Some public schools had dress codes, too, but they were harder to enforce. They didn't have the nuns.

PANTYHOSE MADE THE SCENE

It wasn't until the sixties that pantyhose came to the rescue of ladies everywhere. Imagine being able to throw away the tiresome old garter-belts. Imagine not having to go through the gyrations of pulling on stockings and hooking them front, back, and sides. Now, with panty hose, we had hosiery and underwear all in one garment, easy to slip into, and comfortable for long hours of wear. On a TV interview, Barbara Walters told Gloria Stienam that she took us out of our girdles in the sixties. For that, I thank you, Gloria.

A FASHION SUMMARY

Wars always affect fashion in some way, even if it is only because of shortages. During World War II, fabric was scarce. Dress designers and pattern manufacturers were ordered to create ladies' fashions with certain restrictions. Skirts had to end at the knee. Hems could not be more than two inches; belts no more than two inches. Fabric was needed for military uniforms.

The latest thing in the sixties was an indoor laundry in the kitchen. No more hanging out laundry now that we had those wonderful no-iron fabrics. The housewife is in style herself with her sleeveless sheath, her low heels, and her long straight hair and headband. Is that a "fall" she's wearing?

After the war, designers were no longer restricted. In 1947, Christian Dior created dresses with voluminous calf-length skirts and huge sleeves. Ladies reveled in the luxury of so much fabric, color, and frills. Dior's dresses, with their narrow waists, soft shoulders, and rounded hips, were femininity at its most beautiful. These styles, called the "New Look," were popular throughout the fifties. Going wild with the frilly, frivolous, and feminine, Dior created the A-Line, the H-line, the Trapeze, all extravagant and conspicuous. Other designers were Fath, Balmain, and Balenciaga. CoCo Chanel reopened her Paris shop in 1954, but her trademark was "The Suit." After Dior died, the fashion world was never again entirely led by Paris. Dior's apostle was Givenchy.

In the sixties, designer styles changed to simple, slender, and sleeveless. The pendulum was swinging back again. And with fashion leaders like Jackie Kennedy and Audrey Hepburn, women fell into step like mice following the piper. It's doubtful if the full and frilly fashions will ever return. Women's styles since the sixties have been so easy, so comfortable, and so far from the corsets and garter belts and high heels women endured for centuries, it's hard to think they would return to such misery.

The only thing difficult about fashions in the sixties was the bouffant hairdos. And make-up, especially eye make-up. It takes decades to simplify styles. But by the sixties, we had come a long way since Scarlett O'Hara and her corseted 18-inch waistline. In the sixties, women could at last eat a breakfast roll without belching.

CHAPTER FIFTEEN

The Saints and the Louisiana Superdome

"If the State cannot build a domed stadium, then we should content ourselves with sitting along the banks of the Mississippi River, telling one another what great people we were in grand-daddy's day."

Governor John McKeithen,
addressing New Orleans Chamber of Commerce, 2/2/1966

WE WERE GREAT FOOTBALL FANS, Al and I and our friends. In fact, the people of New Orleans in general were great sports fans, especially of high school and college football, which always drew large crowds. In the late forties and early fifties, Al and I used to take the streetcar on Saturdays to the Tulane stadium, after I got off work at noon from the telephone company. There, we cheered on our local heroes, in heat or cold or driving rain.

Some weekends, when I didn't work on Saturdays, we drove to Baton Rouge with other couples to watch the Tigers and pull for them, so long as they weren't playing Tulane. How exciting it was to hear the Tiger band blaring out their school song as they circled the stadium, whipping the fans up into a frenzy! But as the interest and enthusiasm in professional teams grew, everyone was asking—Why can't New Orleans have a professional football team?

A LONG AND ENVIABLE FOOTBALL HISTORY

Our town had spawned outstanding college teams and players as far back as the twenties. In 1925, the Tulane football team, captained by Lester Lautenschlaeger, won all its games except for a tie with Missouri. Charles "Peggy" Flournoy was named All-American. In 1926, Tulane built a stadium, which was not only the home of the Green Wave, but an arena for every major sports event in New Orleans until the seventies.

Also in 1926, the Loyola Wolfpack had the best record of all major universities in the country. They were undefeated and untied. Their star was Elton "Bucky" Moore, called "The Dixie Flyer."

THE GROWTH OF PRO FOOTBALL

As decades passed and professional football became a national craze, promoters and city officials were more and more determined to have a professional team in New Orleans. Beginning in the late fifties, tireless New Orleans entrepreneur Dave Dixon waged a campaign for a New Orleans professional football franchise. In 1959, he heard that Lamar Hunt, a rich Texan, was about to launch a new professional league, so he contacted Hunt about putting a franchise in New Orleans.

A SAMPLING OF PRO FOOTBALL

In 1960, we got a taste of pro-football when a group called the Louisiana Professional Sports, Inc. promoted an exhibition game for the city. Living just two blocks from City Park Stadium where the game was played, we bought our tickets and walked to the stadium with great anticipation. We were not disappointed. We watched Green Bay defeat Pittsburgh, 20-13, before a crowd of 16,500. In our exodus from the stadium, we heard excited fans all around us expressing their hopes that soon New Orleans would have its own team to cheer on to victory.

Members of the Saints Dance Team who entertained thousands of Saints fans during football season were Gayle Lang, Sharon Sauerbrei, Amy Stanley, and Paula Thibodeaux.

*In some early action against the Atlanta Falcons, former LSU All-American
fullback Jimmy Taylor grinds out a few tough yards with help from Ray
Rissmiller (77) and Joe Wendryhoski (54). (Courtesy New Orleans Saints)*

We read in the paper that Dave Dixon was so inspired by this attendance, he formed a second committee, New Orleans Football Club, Inc., which scheduled an AFL game for City Park Stadium on August 18, 1962. The crowds doubled this time to see the Houston Oilers, featuring former LSU star Billy Cannon, defeat the Boston Patriots 20-10, before a turn-away crowd of 31,000. After that, Dixon received 12,000 pledges for season tickets for a New Orleans team when it became a reality.

NEW ORLEANS GOES PRO!

At last, the day arrived. On November 1, 1966, Rosemary James, reporter for the *States-Item*, wrote a front-page story. "New Orleans scored an economic touchdown today, with the announcement that the city has been awarded a National Football League franchise. The long-awaited announcement," she wrote, "will receive an enthusiastic response from football fans throughout Louisiana and the Gulf Coast area."

A PERMANENT FACILITY IS VITAL

The official announcement had come earlier that day from NFL commissioner Pete Rozelle at a news conference at the Pontchartrain Hotel. He said that all 24 National and American team owners agreed New Orleans was the best spot for the 25th major league football team. Rozelle made it clear in his announcement, however, "that a permanent facility is vital." He was referring to the building of a domed stadium as the team's future home if the proposal was ratified by the electorate.

But on that exciting day, no one was worrying yet about the stadium. In the crowded Patio Room of the beautiful Pontchartrain Hotel, the men seated at a long table, men who had led the pursuit of a NFL team for the city, felt only jubilation. They were Senator Russell Long, Congressman Hale Boggs, Governor John McKeithen, Councilman-at-Large Maurice "Moon" Landrieu representing Mayor Victor Schiro, Tulane University President Dr. Herbert Longenecker, and Bud Adams, owner of the Houston Oilers and member of the NFL expansion committee. Mixing with civic leaders and members of the media was Dave Dixon, the 43-year-old mover and shaker who had inspired and guided the acceptance of a New Orleans team in the NFL.

OUR TEAM NEEDS A NAME

Dave Dixon knew what he wanted to call the team, but he kept it to himself. The *States-Item* newspaper held a contest to find a name for the team. Would it be the Saints? The Tarpons? The Jazz Kings? The final choice would be up to the owners, but to get things going, the newspaper offered a prize for the contest winner, two season tickets for the first season. Of course, the winner was the one who submitted "The Saints," a name taken from the famous New Orleans song, "When the Saints Go Marchin' In."

Dave Dixon tells the story that he was in a restaurant when Archbishop Hannan passed by. Dixon stopped him. "Archbishop," he said, "is it true that it would be a sacrilege to name a football team the Saints?" The Archbishop smiled. "Of course not," he said, "and besides, I have a premonition we're going to need all the help we can get."

So the team was called the Saints. And they would play at Tulane Stadium, which had been committed to them by Darwin S. Fenner, chairman of the Tulane University board, until a new home could be constructed.

19⁶⁷ HOME SCHEDULE

SEPT. 9	ATLANTA FALCONS	8:00 P.M.
SEPT. 17	LOS ANGELES RAMS	1:30 P.M.
SEPT. 24	WASHINGTON REDSKINS	1:30 P.M.
OCT. 1	CLEVELAND BROWNS	1:30 P.M.
OCT. 29	PITTSBURGH STEELERS	1:30 P.M.
NOV. 5	PHILADELPHIA EAGLES	1:00 P.M.
NOV. 12	DALLAS COWBOYS	1:00 P.M.
NOV. 26	ATLANTA FALCONS	1:00 P.M.

Ticket Offices: 944 St. Charles.

1967 HOME SCHEDULE (Courtesy New Orleans Saints)

Model of the Louisiana Superdome and site as planned in the sixties. (Courtesy Curtis & Davis, Architects)

The Louisiana Superdome under construction. It would not be ready for the Saints' football games until 1975, when the cost would have risen from the proposed $46 million to $163 million. The Dome anchored one end of Poydras Street, the Rivergate the other. Note Rivergate backing up ITM Building at the riverfront. (Courtesy Curtis and Davis, Architects)

INTEGRATION AT TULANE STADIUM

For the first time at Tulane Stadium, seating would be integrated. Legal counsel for Dave Dixon's group had drawn up the original articles, knowing that the NFL would not play in a segregated stadium. Until then, there was a section for black fans near the end zone that accommodated about 5,000. That section would be eliminated. Attorney Joe Bernstein remembers. "We hired 250 off-duty New Orleans policemen, brought in a contingent of state troopers, and purchased an insurance policy from Lloyd's of London. Today you look back and think of that time as almost the Stone Age, but then the situation was serious."

In 1965, the AFL scheduled its All-Star game to be played in New Orleans. Sixteen thousand tickets were sold in the first few days. Then 21 black players charged the city with "racism." French Quarter bars refused to serve black players and cab drivers would not take them from the airport to the city. In spite of the efforts of Dave Dixon and Assistant U.S. Attorney Ernest ("Dutch") Morial, later to become New Orleans' first black mayor, the players walked out. But in time tempers cooled and integration was soon accepted, at least at the Saints' games.

BONDS FOR THE LOUISIANA SUPERDOME!

The November 8, 1966, election included voting for bonds to provide money for constructing a domed stadium, the permanent facility that had been referred to as "vital" when New Orleans had been awarded an NFL franchise. The domed stadium's estimated cost was between $30 and $46 million. Proponents of the bond amendment pointed out that it would be a great economic boost for the city. New Orleans would foot the bill by paying a hotel-motel room tax. The *Times-Picayune* and the *States-Item* worked hard for passage. Dixon hit the road, talking up the bonds, making 76 speeches in 46 days. Attendance at the exhibition games had helped in making the decision. The final tally statewide on November 8, 1966, was 5-to-1 in favor of the bond issue. Now the city had a franchise and a stadium (at least on paper).

GOVERNOR McKEITHEN SAYS YES TO THE DOME

The building of the Superdome had the backing of Governor John J. McKeithen. This was essential. Since it was going to cost so much of the state's money and it would seem to be of benefit only to New Orleans, it would never have gone through the state legislature if not for a northern Louisiana Governor who approved it and was willing to push it.

Moon Landrieu was the head of the Domed Stadium Commission, an 11-member board. It turned out to be a much larger stadium than originally planned. And much more expensive. The final cost was $163 million, which was later called "the biggest bargain in history." The stadium moved New Orleans into the major leagues and made us a world-class city.

Before the end of the decade, ground had been broken for the Louisiana Superdome, the "largest room in the world," and it would prove, even at its incredible price, to be worth every cent of the cost.

WHO WANTS TO SPEND $8.5 MILLION?

The prospective owner would have to own 51 percent of the Saints' team. He would also have to be approved by the NFL expansion committee and by

Commissioner Pete Rozelle. Yet the wannabe owners were not scarce. They were crawling out of the woodwork. Rozelle was looking at many wealthy prospective owners, but in 1966, he knew who it would be. There were three solid finalists waiting to spend the big bucks: 1) Jack Sanders, a native Texan, a Marine veteran, and former pro football player; 2) Louis J. Roussel, a banker and developer, who'd made his money in oil; and 3) John Mecom, a 6'4" good looking Texan, whose fortune was somewhere in the half-billion dollar neighborhood. At 27, he would be the youngest owner in the National Football League.

On December 15, 1966, the *States-Item* used big headlines to announce:

"MECOM WINS PRO TEAM FRANCHISE"

TOM FEARS, FIRST HEAD COACH

Tom Fears, former All-Pro receiver for the Los Angeles Rams, was selected head coach for the Saints. Fears had played for the Rams from 1948 to 1956. The forty-year-old had then joined Vince Lombardi briefly on his first staff at Green Bay. He returned to the Rams for two more years, then back to Green Bay, then joined the expansion staff in Atlanta. Now, he and the Saints would combine their strengths for a hopefully bright future.

MIRACLE KICKOFF AT THE FIRST SAINTS GAME

Never in the history of pro-football did an opening kickoff in the first regular game by a brand new team shock the fans more than that of the Saints-Rams game September 17, 1967. The never-to-be-forgotten thrill of a kickoff return of 94 yards for a touchdown by rookie John Gilliam brought wild screams and hysteria from the fans. Was this prophetic of things to come? Were our Saints really this good? Would we go through the season like Super-Saints, wiping out team after team? We wanted to believe it, but were soon disabused of that notion.

There followed some seasons when the Saints' record was so bad the fans wore paper bags on their heads to sit on the Saints' side. Bag heads, they called themselves. On their popular early morning talk show on WSMB Radio, Nut & Jeff (the late Roy Roberts and Jeff Hug) called on the fans to be "Fowl Weather Fans," backing their team no matter what their record was. The Saints were the subject of discussion everywhere: at parties, at work, and on the radio and television. They were our team, and they were followed with great enthusiasm by thousands of New Orleanians.

Throughout the sixties, the Saints' games helped foster integration without bad feelings. Al Hirt was there at every game with his trumpet. Elaborate half-time shows were staged. Cheerleaders and dancers were beautifully costumed and professionally trained. The games brought millions of dollars to the New Orleans economy, especially after the construction of the domed stadium. The Saints helped all us "yats" pull together for an exciting, spirited common cause.

CHAPTER SIXTEEN

The Sixties in Summary

IN THE SIXTIES, we still had Pontchartrain Beach, the playground of the citizens of New Orleans, and it was not just for children, by a long shot. We loved to walk the boardwalk, going on the rides and the amusements. In the Cockeyed Circus, we walked through the tilted room and the mirrored room. In one room, jets of air blew our skirts up and as we grabbed onto them, we suddenly realized viewers were watching us down below and outside the building. We played the machines in the Penny Arcade, asking the gypsy in the glass box to tell our fortunes. My teenagers rode the Zephyr, but by that time my stomach couldn't take the Zephyr any more. We ate soft-serve ice cream and watched the acrobats on the stage set out on the sand.

NEWSPAPERS AND MILK AT OUR DOOR

In the early sixties, we still had our newspaper and milk delivered outside the door in the morning. Back then, paperboys who were willing to get up at 5:00 in the morning threw newspapers from baskets on their bikes.

Before World War II, men had delivered newspapers, but when they were drafted into the military, their routes were shortened and youngsters took their places. Boys continued in these jobs well into the sixties. But by then, the growth in advertising and news coverage increased the size of papers, making them more difficult to carry and to throw. That was when men took over the routes again, tossing the papers at dawn from their car or truck windows.

Most dairies stopped delivering milk to the door in the sixties. They shipped their milk directly to the supermarkets, which kept the milk refrigerated. Of course, it was a better way of handling milk, but I still miss the cream on top of the bottles. I know it isn't good for you, but it was so delicious!

MY FAVORITE MUSIC IN THE SIXTIES

I loved Ricky Nelson strumming his guitar and singing his soft romantic ballads

A typical beauty salon of the sixties was Fashion House on Robert E. Lee Blvd., at West End Blvd. Stylists are, left to right: Willie Francis, Lloyd Buras, Gus Trebucq, and a lovely young lady from Germany named Karol. Bouffant page-boys and French twists were popular hairdos. (Courtesy Judy Pesses)

like "Travelin' Man" and I loved Simon & Garfunkel's haunting "The Sounds of Silence." There were wonderful songs to be heard, even if you weren't a rock fan.

NEIGHBORHOOD SHOWS AND DOWNTOWN STORES

In the sixties, we still had neighborhood shows, and they were listed individually in the daily papers. Movies changed several times a week, and your closest show was usually within walking distance. You didn't have to drive six miles to a building that housed eight theaters to see a movie. This was when we first saw Sean Connery as Bond, James Bond, and the luscious Swedish import, Ann-Margaret, in *Bye-Bye Birdie*.

We still had uptown stores we loved like Maison Blanche, Holmes, Godchaux, Gus Mayer, Krauss, Kress, Imperial Shoe Store, Lerner's, Baker's Shoe Store, and Adler's Jewelry Store. We had wonderful restaurants like Kolb's German Restaurant, Solari's, and Holmes's Restaurant. And we had the beautiful palatial theaters—Loew's, Saenger, and Orpheum—showing first run movies. This choice of nice places to go made it exciting for us to get dressed up on Saturday morning and take the bus to town. It was a treat, whether you had a car or not. It was still "our way" of shopping.

One by one, Canal Street stores began opening branches in the suburbs: Gus Mayer in Gentilly, Maison Blanche in Carrollton, and Holmes in Lakeside Shopping Center. These were stores you drove to and parked free of charge. The shops were moving out to the people, and in time, would leave Canal Street altogether, except for The Gap, which was everywhere.

CARS OF THE SIXTIES

Cars were still long and low, but manufacturers were leaving off the fins and some of the other exterior embellishments of the fifties' cars. The Mercury Cougar had a European flair with concealed headlamps, bucket seats, and a walnut-grained steering wheel. The 1967 Cutlass Supreme had cushy carpets and posh appointments. The Chrysler New Yorker had a passenger recliner. The Volkswagen Station Wagon seated nine and had a sliding sunroof.

The NOW cars from American Motors were the Ambassador, the Rebel, and the Rambler American for styling and safety; the Pontiac 1967 LeMans and the Tempest; the Chevrolet 1967 Caprice for its comfortilt steering wheel; the Plymouth Fury, a two-door hardtop, with safety action inside the door handle.

FAVORITE THINGS OF THE CONSUMER GENERATION

Americans really went for the Polaroid Camera at $19.95. It took black and white pictures and was called The Swinger. Also a must if you had children was the Kodak Instamatic Movie Camera and Projector.

The aluminum can came on the market in 1960, the tab can in 1963. Also in 1960, the felt tip pen became available.

Between 1961 and 1966, new conveniences came on the market such as the self-wringing mop, electric toothbrush, home video recorder, push-button telephone, electric carving knife, and the disposable photographic four-shot flash cube.

Partygoers acted as if they'd just invented vodka. They used it mainly in Martinis, the alcoholic beverage of choice in the sixties, but also in Bloody Marys.

Everybody still smoked cigarettes in the sixties. Pall Mall offered "the long

Open house on a Sunday afternoon in New Orleans East in the sixties. Ranch-style suburban houses in three designs.

cigarette that was long on flavor." Belair was a filter tipped cigarette with a light menthol taste. Raleigh also had a filter tip. Salem had the menthol taste.

Packaged food was the ideal way around cooking. We could get Knorr soup in a boxed package in onion or vegetable flavors. Frozen TV dinners offered chopped sirloin with French fries, peas, and a blueberry muffin. Remember Sealtest Checkerboard Ice Cream? How in the world did they do that?

EVENTS IN NEW ORLEANS BY YEARS

In 1962, the Catholic schools of New Orleans integrated

In 1963, we lost a president and a pope. President Kennedy, 1,000 days in office, had pushed for civil rights legislation, but didn't live to see it passed. Pope John XXIII called the Second Vatican Council which "opened the windows of the church." Vatican II made changes in the church such as saying the mass in English.

Public housing projects, then battered and boarded, were being hailed as the way to get low-income families in New Orleans out of the slums. Guste Homes near Pontchartrain Expressway were opened.

1963 ended and 1964 began with "the snow of the century," 3.8 inches of snow.

In 1964, (March), the ITM Building was still a hole in the ground at the foot of Canal Street. Ambassador Chep Morrison and his seven-year-old son Randy were killed in a plane crash in Mexico.

On May 30, the Canal Streetcar made its last trip down the widest thoroughfare in the world. New Orleanians grieved to see an end come to the familiar landmark, the rocking Toonerville Trolley we had all grown up with. It was replaced by buses, which were supposed to be an environmental improvement, but required the removal of miles of tracks, and the pouring of miles of cement on which the buses would run.

In June, President Lyndon B. Johnson signed the Civil Rights Act into law. The Plaza Tower was scheduled to be 12 stories higher than the ITM Building.

Archbishop Joseph Francis Rummel, 88, died after a long illness. Named as Apostolic Administrator for the Archdiocese was John Patrick Cody.

The Beatles played at City Park, and Beatlemania broke out.

Hap Glaudi, local sportscaster, had a role in a *Gunsmoke* episode.

In 1965, (September 9), Hurricane Betsy visited the city with winds up to 173 mph. And into these winds came Archbishop Philip M. Hannan, who had given the eulogy at President Kennedy's funeral. He was to be the new Archbishop of New Orleans.

In 1967, the Saints sold 35,900 season tickets for their first season.

In 1968, (April 4) Civil Rights leader Martin Luther King was killed by an assassin's bullet in Memphis, Tennessee. Archbishop Philip Hannan mourned his death with a Mass at the St. Louis Cathedral. Senator Robert F. Kennedy was shot down in a hotel kitchen, as he left after giving a speech in his campaign for the presidency.

ADVANCES IN MEDICINE AND TECHNOLOGY

The use of the birth-control pill became widespread in the sixties. More than any other single invention, it caused major changes in the lifestyle and outlook of women on sex. They became more casual about having intercourse without marriage, and with more than one partner. Without fear of conceiving, they were liberated. They were no longer dependent upon men.

Beautiful kitchen and dinette of the sixties. Fully automatic built-in appliances saved space and made the home modern and efficient. Natural wood tabletops and hutch made it homey.

Few houses were built on speculation in the sixties without a den and a wet bar.
Bar stools, fireplace, and lighted bookcase added to décor.

In 1960, the first artificial kidney was developed. A pacemaker was developed to control heartbeat.

In 1962, the first eye surgery was performed by laser.

In 1963, the first home video recorder was demonstrated in London. Valium, a tranquilizer, was developed. It became the world's most widely used tranquilizer.

In 1964, the first picturephone system, combining television and telephone was demonstrated by AT&T at the New York World's Fair. The first public demonstration of satellite television feed via stationary satellite allowed the Tokyo Olympic games to be relayed to North America.

In 1965, the first soft contact lenses were developed. The Medicare system began in the United States.

In 1967, the first coronary bypass operation was introduced by American surgeon Rene Favalero. South African surgeon Christiaan N. Barnard performed the first heart transplant. His patient lived for 18 days. His second transplant patient (1968) lived 74 days.

In 1968, enzymes that could cut DNA strands at specific points were discovered. They would later help make genetic engineering possible.

In 1969, *Apollo 11* successfully landed the first men on the moon. On their return, the astronauts traveled from moon orbit faster than any human beings ever before. The first television broadcast from the moon reached 100 million viewers by satellite feed.

TURMOIL AND TECHNOLOGY

In the sixties, New Orleans was on an economic roll. Poydras Street became a new and beautiful avenue leading to the river, lined with huge, magnificent buildings, each of which housed businesses that employed thousands. It was a decade that saw the rise of the Rivergate, the ITM Building, the new Civil Courts Building, and the beginning of the 30-year plan to turn the Port of New Orleans into Centroport, U.S.A. It saw the completion of ten buildings on the campus of LSUNO (now UNO). Yet the city of New Orleans, like many other big cities in the sixties, was undergoing revolution by every minority that suffered discrimination. Doors were opening for them, but forces were resisting, and everyone felt the tension.

Television, the most popular form of entertainment ever yet devised, mirrored the Generation Gap and tried to find new ways to appeal to the youth of America. Rock music brought young people together in mobs and encouraged them to rebel, and the Vietnam War tore families apart. Life was not simple in the sixties. But the baby boomers who made all the noise and burned their draft cards would in time be husbands and fathers and home owners and taxpayers with jobs and responsibilities, and they'd look back on the times they'd defied the Establishment and hope to God their sons would never do the same.

INDEX